# Disney
Winnie the Pooh

The Hundred-Acre Wood Cookbook

Disney
Winnie the Pooh

The Hundred-Acre Wood
Cookbook

Family-Friendly Recipes Featuring Eeyore,
Kanga, Roo, Tigger, Rabbit, Piglet, Owl,
and Most of All Winnie the Pooh

Recipes by Vivian Jao and Liz Tarpy
Written by James Asmus

SAN RAFAEL • LOS ANGELES • LONDON

Contents

7   Food and Friends in the Hundred-Acre Wood
8   A Word on Cooking with Kids

Chapter 1
All About Honey

15 Pooh Bear Pancakes with Honey-Berry Compote
17 Chocolate-Dipped Honeycomb Sweets
21 Trio of Flavoured Honeys
22 Honeyed Yoghurt Parfait with Quinoa, Pomegranate Seeds, and Grapes
25 Honey Nut Granola
26 Orange and Almond Scones with Honey Butter
29 Corn on the Cob with Whipped Honey-Miso Butter
30 Walnut Baklava
33 Honey Apple Cupcakes with Honey Soft Cream Cheese Frosting
37 Honey-Poached Pears
38 Honey Lemonade with Mint Ice Cubes

Chapter 2
Parties and Picnics

43 Hero Cake
47 Dirt Cake Trifle
49 Thumbprint Biscuits
52 Open-Faced Radish and Herbed Cheese Tea Sandwiches
55 Cucumber, Dill, and Avocado Pressed Rice Sandwiches
59 Haycorn Tea
60 Coronation Chicken Sliders
63 Smoked Trout Dip
64 Creamy Potato Salad with Pickled Mustard Seeds and Spring Onions
67 Salted Watermelon Punch with Cucumber and Basil

Chapter 3
Rabbit's Garden

71 Wedge Salad with Carrot-Ginger Dressing
72 Sugar Snap Peas, Watercress, and Mint Salad
75 Smashed Celery Salad with Grainy Mustard Dressing
76 Green Couscous
79 Grilled Asparagus with Green Goddess Dressing
80 Eeyore's Rainbow Veggie and Hummus Tray
83 Tomato and Herbed Ricotta Galette
86 Smoked Paprika Baked Acorn Squash
89 Veggie Chilli-Stuffed Jacket Potatoes
90 Trio of Quick Pickles
93 Rabbit's Smoothie

Chapter 4
Holidays in the Hundred-Acre Wood

- 97 Guava and Soft Cream Cheese Hearts
- 99 Chocolate Bark with Pretzels and Dried Cranberries
- 101 Beetroot-Dyed Deviled Eggs
- 103 Basque Cheesecake with Orange Blossom Honey
- 106 Witches' Brew
- 109 Eeyore's 'Thistle' Soup
- 110 Stilton Toasts with Roasted Grapes
- 113 Cauliflower Cheese with Pretzel Crust
- 115 Pizzelle Snowflakes
- 119 Roasted Vegetable Platter with Honey Butter Glaze
- 120 Lemon Posset Glazed with Marmalade

Chapter 5
Suppers

- 125 Mushrooms on Toast
- 126 Cheese and Onion Pie
- 129 Asparagus, Potato, and Pecorino Frittata
- 133 Za'atar Roasted Chickpeas, Butternut Squash, and Red Onions with Lime Yoghurt
- 134 Sweetcorn and Potato Chowder
- 137 Fusilli Pasta with Pistachio Pesto and Peas
- 139 Chilli Cornbread Casserole
- 140 Grilled Salmon with Honey-Coriander Glaze

Chapter 6
Smackerels

- 145 Piglet's Big Goat's Cheese Log
- 146 Pimiento Cheese Toasties
- 149 Crumpet Antipasti Pizza
- 150 Fresh Cabbage Pancakes
- 153 Pooh's Pasties
- 154 Tigger-Striped Biscuits
- 158 Haycorns
- 161 Eeyore's Tails
- 162 Malted Ice-Cream Sundae with Mini Malted Mochi
- 165 Kiwi and Strawberry Ice Lollies
- 166 Avocado Milk Shake

168 Ingredients and Methods
172 About the Authors
173 Index

Food and Friends in the Hundred-Acre Wood

Just beyond the horizon lies the Hundred-Acre Wood. This wondrous place is where a young boy named Christopher Robin ventures to visit his many dear friends—dearest amongst them being Winnie the Pooh.

If you know anything of Pooh, likely it is that he is a small yellow bear who is terribly fond of honey. ('Terribly' as in 'very' and also 'occasionally gets him into terrible trouble with bees.') So it is a great kindness then when Christopher Robin (or any friend) shares a bit of honey to save him the trouble.

In fact, food is often an act of kindness in these woods. Whether bringing some thistles to cheer up gloomy Eeyore or offering some home-cooked comfort to a worried Piglet, the residents here know how sharing a meal can brighten a rainy day. In times of celebration, Tigger enjoys dishes prepared in his honour (whether they were intended that way or not).

Roo and his doting mother, Kanga, play together in the kitchen to make tasty holiday gifts for their friends. And every picnic is a showcase for Rabbit to serve the fruits (and vegetables) of his (very) serious labours in his prized garden.

Though a meal is just one short thing to be shared—like a laugh, a thanks, or an adventure—with how often Pooh Bear gets rumbly in the tumbly, it may be the simplest and most ready way to offer a bit of care and connection to those you hold dear.

And now Pooh, Christopher Robin, and all the others are happy to welcome you to join in the fun and share some of these moments. So in the times apart from one another, you can make these reminders of your friends in the Hundred-Acre Wood to share with friends elsewhere—whether inviting someone for supper, preparing a very special party, or simply sharing a small smackerel of something.

A Word on Cooking with Kids

by Vivian Jao

There is a whole world of food to explore, and cooking with kids is one of the best ways to begin that adventure. Involving kids with cooking encourages them to try new foods, which is helpful if the little ones are fussy or reluctant eaters. Cooking is an essential life skill, so take advantage of a child's curiosity early. Kids often want to know what is causing the clatter and good smells coming out of the kitchen. Learning to cook is one of the first steps in teaching kids to be independent and to feel empowered. It boosts their self-confidence and self-esteem. There is a lot of pride to be had in sharing a dish you've made with friends and family. They want to be involved—embrace it!

When cooking with kids, you may sometimes feel as frustrated as Rabbit is with Pooh and their friends. Try to channel Kanga's patience and calmness and enjoy the experience. (Also, see Kanga and Roo on page 10 for a selection of recipes that may be easiest to cook with little ones.) Keep in mind that cooking allows kids to be creative and artistic. Let kids help pick out dishes to cook, whether they're old favourites or new ones!

Photos from cookbooks or websites and even cooking shows can get them excited. Encourage kids to experiment—swap ingredients, vegetables, herbs, spices, toppings, and garnishes. Kids will learn that not all flavour combos work, that mistakes will happen, and that it's not the end of the world. The journey is just as important as the final dish. They'll learn and appreciate the effort it takes to cook and to be kind both to themselves and others, which is always a good thing.

Cooking is a sensory activity that also engages sight, smell, touch, hearing, and, finally and most importantly, taste. Describe textures so they learn to recognise them. Season and taste as you go, so they can see how the flavours build and change. Cooking is a tactile, hands-on experience that teaches hand-eye coordination and develops fine motor skills. Engage them—allow them to take part as much as possible depending on their age and capabilities. Hands are the most useful tools in the kitchen. If the recipe allows, let them get their *clean* hands involved in washing vegetables, tearing lettuce, picking herbs, kneading, shaping, forming, mixing, assembling, and sprinkling. When they're ready, let them use graters and knives or actually help cook at the hob. Start with simple dishes, or, if making something more complicated, allow them to take part in the easier steps and slowly move on to more complicated ones.

Learning to cook teaches kids how to follow instructions and be collaborative. Have them add ingredients, stir, set and keep an eye on the timer, measure, roll out, cut, and even cook when they're ready. Kids learn delayed gratification while waiting for food to cook and cool. Cooking involves maths, chemistry, nutrition, and health. It can foster a positive relationship with food early on. Kids can learn about budgeting (expensive ingredients and cost-effective choices), where food comes from, sustainability, and different cultures. You can even share family history and traditions to form connections with food.

WHEN COOKING WITH KIDS, SET YOURSELF UP FOR SUCCESS:

Start with a clean and clear working space. It doesn't necessarily need to be on a table or counter. Baking trays on an oilcloth or coated tablecloth on the kitchen floor work well with the little ones, too!

- Have the recipe easily accessible.

- Have all tools, utensils, measuring and cooking equipment, and towels out.

- Pull out all the ingredients before starting and place them in the order they need to be used. Put them aside as used. This way, you can see early on if you forgot to include any ingredient in the dish.

- Measure each ingredient into a separate bowl before adding or mixing it into the larger bowl of ingredients. This way, if the child's hands are a bit shaky, or they spill, or if they make a mistake, it can easily be caught and fixed. You can start again with that ingredient without messing up the entire dish. (This is especially helpful when separating eggs.)

- To prevent waste, place the bowl on a clean larger plate or baking tray to catch any excess of the ingredient being measured. The excess can then be poured back into the original container. Or, if the child is overly enthusiastic when mixing and food is spilling out of the bowl, the food can easily be added back to the bowl. It also makes cleanup easier.

- Tidy up as you go and clean up when you're done.

Remember to always supervise the little ones, from measuring ingredients to eventually working with sharp utensils. Keep pot handles turned in, where curious hands can't reach. Teach them to be cautious around hot pots and tins and even food. Keep kids away from the hot hob and oven until they've learned how to work safely around them and gained a healthy level of caution. Scrapes, cuts, and burns are inevitable accidents in cooking, even for adults, but don't let that discourage them.

Cooking together creates memories: the many successful attempts that have them beaming with pride, as well as the ones you can laugh at when a dish turns out to be a very horrible mess, and the heroic attempts to save a dish. Make cooking with little ones fun, and your engagement, encouragement, and support may instill curiosity, nurture skills, and foster self-reliance for a lifetime.

Kanga and Roo

'Come along now, Roo.'
'Yes, Mama!'

The loving mother and son Kanga and Roo always bring their nurturing kindness and adventurous spirit. Those qualities combine when they enjoy an afternoon together in the kitchen, trying out new dishes to share with their friends. If you are hopping into the kitchen with your own little one, these recipes are especially welcoming or collaborative.

Look for the flower icon on these two pages if you want to find the easiest of the kid-friendly recipes.

All About Honey

- **Trio of Flavoured Honeys (page 21)**
  Put flavourings into the jars.
- **Honeyed Yoghurt Parfait with Quinoa, Pomegranate Seeds, and Grapes (page 22)**
  Pick the pomegranate seeds (very messy but fun!), cut the grapes, whisk the honey mixture, and assemble the parfait layers.
- **Honey Nut Granola (page 25)**
  Measure and mix the oats, nuts, and seeds and break the cooled granola into clusters.
- **Honey Apple Cupcakes with Honey Soft Cream Cheese Frosting (page 33)**
  Whisk the dry ingredients, add batter ingredients to the stand mixer, fold in grated apples, fill cupcake liners with batter, and frost the cupcakes.
- **Honey Lemonade with Mint Ice Cubes (page 38)**
  Put mint leaves in ice cube trays, juice the lemons, and mix the lemonade.

Parties and Picnics

- **Dirt Cake Trifle (page 47)**
  Pick out the nicest small strawberries for garnish, coat the strawberries with melted candy melts, crush graham crackers (if not using a food processor), and layer ingredients.
- **Thumbprint Biscuits (page 49)**
  Roll the dough into balls and in the sugar, make indents, and fill with jam.
- **Open-Faced Radish and Herbed Cheese Tea Sandwiches (page 52)**
  Spread the cheese and top with radishes.
- **Smoked Trout Dip (page 63)**
  Mix the dip ingredients and break the trout into flakes.

Rabbit's Garden

- **Smashed Celery Salad with Grainy Mustard Dressing (page 75)**
  Mix the vinaigrette, pick celery leaves, smash the celery (if not using a knife), and toss it all together.

- **Eeyore's Rainbow Veggie and Hummus Tray (page 80)**
  Arrange the veggies in a rainbow shape.

- **Trio of Quick Pickles (page 90)**
  Put the prepared vegetables and flavouring ingredients into the jars.

- **Rabbit's Smoothie (page 93)**
  Add the ingredients to the blender.

Holidays in the Hundred-Acre Wood

- **Guava and Soft Cream Cheese Hearts (page 97)**
  Cut out hearts, stack the guava and soft cream cheese, seal the hearts with a fork, brush them with egg wash, and sprinkle with sugar.

- **Chocolate Bark with Pretzels and Dried Cranberries (page 99)**
  Press pretzels and fruit into the bark and break the bark into pieces once firm.

- **Witches' Brew (page 106)**
  Put the gummy worms in the ice mould and pour in the juice and ginger ale.

Suppers

- **Za'atar Roasted Chickpeas, Butternut Squash, and Red Onions with Lime Yoghurt (page 133)**
  Rinse, drain, and dry the chickpeas, toss the chickpeas and veggies with seasoning and arrange on the baking tray, and mix the lime yoghurt.

- **Grilled Salmon with Honey-Coriander Glaze (page 140)**
  Grind coriander seeds in a mortar and pestle, mix the glaze, arrange the salmon on the baking tray, and brush the plated salmon with the glaze.

Smackerels

- **Piglet's Big Goat's Cheese Log (page 145)**
  Roll the cheese in nuts and herbs.

- **Crumpet Antipasti Pizza (page 149)**
  Add sauce, cheese, and toppings to pizzas.

- **Pooh's Pasties (page 153)**
  Brush the pasties with egg wash and top with dough circles and legs to form Pooh's backside.

- **Tigger-Striped Biscuits (page 154)**
  Layer the buscuit dough to form stripes (uneven and messy is good here).

- **Malted Ice-Cream Sundae with Mini Malted Mochi (page 162)**
  Dust the work surface and mochi with cornflour, cut the mochi into squares (using a plastic knife), pull the mochi apart and toss in the cornflour and sift, toss the mochi in malted milk powder, and assemble the sundaes.

- **Kiwi and Strawberry Ice Lollies (page 165)**
  Cut the strawberries and kiwis and squeeze the lime juice.

Chapter 1

All About Honey

A day with Winnie the Pooh will most certainly become a day of enjoying honey.

A person spending many a day with Pooh, however, may begin to crave a bit more variety in their mealtimes.

Fortunately, honey can liven up all sorts of dishes and delights. So whether your tummy is rumbling for a tasty treat or a hearty helping of more filling foods, a smartly applied bit of that sweet and sticky stuff can have both you and Pooh feeling satisfied.

(And if you have a full day's honey sorted, Pooh will gladly accompany you on any adventure you have in mind.)

Pooh Bear Pancakes with Honey-Berry Compote

Upon rising, Pooh will, of course, be hungry for honey. But even a boy as young as Christopher Robin can tell you that persons require more sustenance for a full day of adventure. Fortunately, this relatively simple recipe provides a hearty breakfast no less bursting with awakening flavour. In this case, the bright sweetness of honey is only deepened by blending into the gooey richness of berry compote cooked with cinnamon. Just be sure to apply enough to complement your warm and fluffy pancakes before Pooh gets his paws on the mix.

YIELD: 4 servings (eight 10-centimetre pancakes)

COMPOTE
One 425-gram bag frozen mixed berries, thawed

NOTE: *Berries in season? You'll need more of them to make the compote, and the sauce will take longer to cook, but it's a great option.*

60 grams honey
Zest of 1 small lemon
0.6 gram ground cinnamon
Pinch kosher (coarse) salt

PANCAKES
15 millilitres freshly squeezed lemon juice
475 millilitres milk
42 grams unsalted butter, plus more for the tray as needed
240 grams plain flour
25 grams sugar
11.5 grams baking powder
4.6 grams bicarbonate of soda
3.3 grams kosher (coarse) salt
1 large egg, beaten
Fresh berries, to garnish

To make the compote: In a medium saucepan over a medium-high heat, combine the berries, honey, lemon zest, cinnamon, and salt and bring to a simmer. Lower the heat to maintain a gentle simmer until most of the liquid evaporates and the compote thickens, about 15 minutes. Keep warm until serving.

To make the pancakes: Preheat the oven to 95°C. Fit a baking tray with a wire rack.

In a medium bowl, stir the lemon juice into the milk. This will create some lumps and provide the acid needed to activate the bicarbonate of soda to make fluffy pancakes. (If you prefer to just use buttermilk, go for it!)

Put the butter in a ramekin, cover, and microwave until melted, about 20 seconds. Let cool while you prepare the rest of the ingredients.

While the milk thickens, in a large bowl, whisk together the flour, sugar, baking powder, bicarbonate of soda, and salt.

Add the egg and melted butter to the milk and whisk to combine. Pour the wet ingredients into the dry ingredients and gently whisk just until combined with a few floury lumps (you want to avoid overmixing or your pancakes will be chewy).

Heat a large non-stick griddle or frying pan over a medium heat until a splash of water dances and sizzles on the surface, about 5 minutes. Ladle about 60 millilitres of the batter into the centre of the pan and use the bottom of the ladle to create a circle about 10 centimetres in diameter for Pooh's head. Use a spoon to make two small rounds of batter, at 11 o'clock and 1 o'clock, for his ears. Cook until the edges look a little dry, the bottom is golden brown, and bubbles dot the surface, about 1½ minutes. Flip and continue to cook until browned on the other side, another 1 to 2 minutes. Transfer to the prepared baking tray and keep warm in the oven while you make the remaining pancakes.

Serve the pancakes with the warm berry compote. Garnish with fresh berries as desired.

Winnie the Pooh

'I've got a rumbly in my tumbly.'

If one thing is certain in the Hundred-Acre Wood, it is that the friendly little bear Winnie the Pooh will be glad to see you, and have your company.

The next thing to be certain of is that he will likely, in some short amount of time, inquire as to whether it is time to eat a little something.

Then thirdly (though no less certain), Pooh Bear will insist that any morsel of sustenance contain a fortifying amount of honey.

So if one is intending to enjoy an adventure through the woods, consider bringing something from this chapter to share. With an assortment of recipes to choose from, you shall likely find something or other to your tastes—yet each features enough of that golden deliciousness to satisfy the pickiest of small yellow bears.

The final certainty is that, in sharing, your palate and your friendship will be all the sweeter for it.

Chocolate-Dipped Honeycomb Sweets

Truth be told, Winnie the Pooh had thought he would like to carry a pot of honey with him at all times. Yet the unfortunate fact remains that oftentimes it simply is not polite for one to be All Sticky.

Fortunately for Pooh (and you?) honey is easily turned into Chocolate-Dipped Honeycomb Sweets. With all the sweetness and rich, unmistakable flavour of its gooier form, this hardened and airier honey can be picked up and enjoyed without creating the same sort of mess. What's more, honeycomb can be made even more of a treat by coating it with chocolate—either dark (to temper and complexify the sweetness) or milk (to double the sweetness), which is, of course, Pooh's preference.

YIELD: About 50 pieces (depending on the size of the pieces)

- Non-stick cooking spray (optional)
- 18.4 grams bicarbonate of soda
- 300 grams sugar
- 160 grams honey
- 60 millilitres water, plus more for brushing
- 240 to 350 millilitres milk chocolate or bittersweet chocolate, chopped

SPECIAL TOOLS
- Small fine-mesh sieve
- Pastry brush
- Digital instant-read thermometer or sugar thermometer

Tips for Success
- Keep the kids at a safe distance until the honeycomb is completely cooled. Hot sugar can cause serious burns.
- Save the smaller pieces and crumbs to decorate Honey Apple Cupcakes with Honey Soft Cream Cheese Frosting (page 33), top ice cream, or mix into coffee.
- To clean the sticky pan, fill the pan with water and bring to a simmer. The hardened sugar will dissolve into the heated water.

Line a baking tray with non-stick baking paper. If your baking paper is not slick and slippery, lightly oil it with cooking spray so the sweets can be peeled off without sticking.

Have the following within reach of the hob before you start cooking: bicarbonate of soda with a small fine-mesh sieve, a whisk, a small bowl of water with a pastry brush, a digital instant-read or sugar thermometer, a rubber spatula, and the prepared tray.

In a 3.3- to 3.8-litre high-sided, heavy-based saucepan over a medium heat, combine the sugar, honey, and water. Bring to the boil, brushing down the sides of the pan with water to prevent crystals forming, and whisking gently until the sugar dissolves.

Stop stirring and carefully attach the thermometer to the side of the pan. The syrup will bubble up and then cook down low in the pan, so make sure the tip of the thermometer is close to but not touching the bottom of the pan. Continue to cook without whisking until the thermometer reaches 150°C.

Continued on page 19.

All About Honey

Remove the pot from the heat and carefully remove the thermometer. Sift the bicarbonate of soda into the pot and whisk vigorously until it's mixed in, 10 to 15 seconds. Be careful while doing so, as the mixture will quickly foam up and expand in the pan. Use a rubber spatula to scrape it onto the prepared baking tray. Do not spread it with the spatula or the bubbles will flatten. Set the tray aside and let the honeycomb cool completely, about 30 minutes. The honeycomb will deflate a bit as it cools. Peel the honeycomb off the baking paper and return it to the baking tray. Use the tip of a knife or your hands to break the honeycomb into pieces. Line two baking trays with baking paper and set aside.

In a medium microwave-safe bowl, melt the chocolate in the microwave in 30-second intervals, stirring after each interval, about 1½ minutes total. Dip the honeycomb pieces partially into the chocolate and transfer them to the prepared baking tray to set. Store in an airtight container at room temperature for three days.

Fun Facts

- Airy, crisp, and crunchy, honeycomb in its various forms is known worldwide by many names—honeycomb toffee, cinder toffee, sponge toffee, hokey pokey, sponge candy, fairy food sweets, seafoam, and dalgona, amongst others.
- Whisking bicarbonate of soda into the hot syrup causes the syrup to billow up and expand, creating air pockets in the honeycomb.

Replenishing Your Honey Supply

If one is to make several of these recipes, one will likely empty one's cupboard of honey. Luckily, Pooh was happy to share his method for gathering more!

STEP 1: Obtain a balloon (the floaty kind).

STEP 2: Roll yourself in mud until you resemble a little rain cloud.

STEP 3: Float on the balloon up to the beehive in a honey tree.

STEP 4: Reach in for handfuls of honey.

Should the bees grow suspicious, have an associate open an umbrella and loudly suggest, 'Tut-tut, it looks like rain!'

Trio of Flavoured Honeys

Even a creature of Very Particular Tastes such as Winnie the Pooh occasionally hungers for variety. In such moments of unusual abandon, that mostly means Pooh may experiment with *flavoured* honey.

Should you find yourself feeling just as daring as our friend, each of these three infusions will add exciting new dimension to your honey cupboard—and an easy way to add dynamic new dimension to recipes . . . or your next smackerel of sweetness straight from the jar.

YIELD: Three 240-millilitre jars flavoured honey

5.6 grams crushed chillies
1 large fresh rosemary sprig, cut to fit the jar
1 vanilla pod, halved and seeds scraped
720 grams honey

SPECIAL TOOLS
Three clean and dry 240-millilitre airtight jars

Tips for Success (and Safety!)

- The jars and utensils need to be clean and dry, and the flavourings used to infuse the honey have to have minimal to zero moisture or the honey may spoil.
- If you see mould or the honey smells musty, discard.
- Though it's tempting, avoid using your fingers to clean off any drips.

Put the crushed chillies into one jar, the rosemary into a second jar, and the vanilla pod and seeds into the third.

Heat the honey in a small saucepan over a low heat just until loose and warm to the touch (or microwave in a liquid measuring cup in 30-second increments).

Fill each jar with 240 grams of honey (or about to the top of each jar). Seal the jars and let them sit to infuse for at least two days, or longer if you desire greater heat from the crushed chillies or a deeper rosemary or vanilla flavour. Taste the honey each day until it's to your liking.

Strain out the crushed chillies if desired (heat the honey a little in the microwave to loosen it so it pours and strains more easily). Remove the rosemary sprig and vanilla pod if desired. Stir the vanilla honey before using, as the seeds will eventually migrate to the top. The infused honeys will keep for a couple of months stored at room temperature.

Honeyed Yoghurt Parfait with Quinoa, Pomegranate Seeds, and Grapes

Young Roo, if one takes his word for it, is ready for anything. Be it swimming, bouncing, exploring, or staying up very, very late—Roo would even prefer to enjoy it all in one day. Considering this ambition, Kanga starts him off with a breakfast suited to keep any child (or visiting friends) energised for a full day of adventure.

This packed parfait fits the bill perfectly—layering practically a full breakfast of bright fresh fruits, tart yoghurt, earthy quinoa, and sweet honey. Though the elements can be easily substituted (with other favourite fruits, or whichever are on hand), quinoa is particularly packed with protein, fibre, and nutrients to help keep Roo (or anyone else) hopping through the day.

YIELD: 4 servings

85 grams uncooked quinoa
240 millilitres water
475 grams natural Greek yoghurt
40 grams honey
2 grams freshly grated lime zest
150 grams quartered or halved seedless grapes
90 grams pomegranate seeds

Tips for Success

- If making this for young children, make sure to quarter the grapes rather than halving them.
- Quinoa is coated with a natural compound, saponin, which tastes bitter if not washed off.
- It's not easy to cook less than 85 grams of quinoa, so you'll have some quinoa left over. Save the remainder for another batch of parfaits or for a grain bowl.

Put the quinoa into a fine-mesh sieve and thoroughly rinse it with water, moving the seeds around with your fingers. Drain well and put into a medium saucepan. Add the water and bring to the boil over a high heat. Reduce the heat to maintain a simmer, cover, and cook until all the water is absorbed, about 10 minutes. Set the quinoa aside to cool, then fluff it with a fork.

In a medium bowl, whisk together the yoghurt, honey, and lime zest. Layer in each of four glasses, in the following order: 45 grams yoghurt, 11.5 grams quinoa, 37.5 grams grapes, 45 grams yoghurt, 11.5 grams quinoa, and 22.5 grams pomegranate seeds.

Serve immediately or cover and refrigerate until ready to eat.

Honey Nut Granola

Then there is the matter of Piglet. Knowing himself to be such a small and timid fellow, he would forgive you if you had forgotten about him completely. Yet he is not forgotten, especially by Winnie the Pooh. You can show your own consideration of both with a lovely mix of homemade granola such as this. The flavourful assortment of nuts and seeds can save Piglet the worry of foraging for the day's haycorns. (The coating of honey, naturally, invites Pooh.) And the delightful play between the sweet and salty elements and seasoning reminds us that those special friends who provide balance to us are, in fact, delightfully unforgettable.

YIELD: About 950 grams

- 56 grams unsalted butter
- 160 grams honey
- 70 grams dark brown sugar
- 0.8 gram kosher (coarse) salt
- 200 grams old-fashioned oats
- 100 grams pecans
- 130 grams pumpkin seeds
- 140 grams shelled sunflower seeds
- 97.5 grams soft apricots

Preheat the oven to 180°C, or gas mark 4. Line a baking tray with baking paper or a silicone mat and set aside.

In a medium saucepan over a medium heat, melt the butter. Add the honey, sugar, and salt and cook, stirring occasionally, until the sugar dissolves.

Meanwhile, in a large bowl, mix the oats, pecans, pumpkin seeds, and sunflower seeds. Add the honey mixture to the oat mixture and mix well to coat evenly. Spread the granola in a single layer on the prepared baking tray. Bake, stirring every 10 minutes, until the granola is golden brown, 20 to 25 minutes.

Let the granola cool. Break it into clusters and stir in the apricots.

All About Honey

Orange and Almond Scones with Honey Butter

Kanga, like many caretakers, has learned a great deal about food and its effects. One insight she could tell you is that, when caring for several appetites at once, the job is easier if you can avoid arguments over whether someone got more. Though Roo may be her only child, her heart is full enough to care for all her friends and loved ones. So recipes such as this allow Kanga (or you, if you'd like) to hand out one lovingly made, lightly sweet-and-savoury scone to each outstretched paw. These densely satisfying snacks (or breakfast staples) also offer such a range of subtle flavours—orange zest, light nutty finish, and a drench of rich honey butter—that tummies and tempers are tamed in no time.

YIELD: 8 scones

HONEY BUTTER
113 grams (1 stick) unsalted butter, at room temperature
100 grams honey

SCONES
240 grams plain flour, plus more for dusting
37.5 grams sugar
9.2 grams baking powder
1.65 grams kosher (coarse) salt
113 grams (1 stick) unsalted butter, chilled, cut into tiny bits
180 millilitres double cream
1 large egg
Zest of 1 large orange
Flaked almonds, for garnish

SPECIAL TOOLS
Electric whisk (optional)
Food processor (optional)
Pastry brush

To make the honey butter: In a medium bowl, use an electric whisk to whip the butter and honey until fluffy. (You can also just mix by hand with a rubber spatula or wooden spoon.)

To make the scones: Preheat the oven to 200°C, or gas mark 6. Line a baking tray with baking paper or a silicone mat.

In a food processor or large bowl, pulse or whisk the flour, sugar, baking powder, and salt to combine. Drop the bits of butter into the flour and pulse or use two knives or a pastry blender to incorporate the butter into the flour just until it resembles coarse cornmeal. Don't let it turn into a paste.

Measure the cream into a 475-millilitre liquid measuring cup and then whisk the egg and orange zest into the cream. Pour into the food processor and pulse just until the mixture barely comes together into a soft dough. It will be a little sticky.

Turn the dough onto a lightly floured surface and sprinkle the top with a little flour as well. Gently knead just until the dough comes together into a smooth ball. Pat the dough into a 15- to 18-centimetre diameter, 2-centimetre-thick disk. Cut into eight wedges and arrange 2.5 centimetres or so apart on the prepared baking tray. Brush the tops with some of the honey butter. Firmly press the almonds into the dough to adhere, either flat or at an angle. Bake until lightly golden on the bottoms and edges, about 15 minutes.

Serve warm slathered with more honey butter.

Corn on the Cob with Whipped Honey-Miso Butter

In which we are reminded that a nice thing may still be made even better.

Rabbit, naturally, loves few things more than a perfectly grown vegetable. Pooh, as is well-known, loves no food so much as honey. The resulting challenge for poor Rabbit has been how to be an abiding host to his friend Pooh, when the time calls for nourishment—but Rabbit still prefers things Just So.

On one such occasion, Rabbit wanted nothing more than to savour some freshly picked, perfectly grown ears of sweetcorn. Pooh, of course, wanted honey. After some great kerfuffle in Rabbit's kitchen (the cause of which, I'm afraid, I have now forgotten), the perfectly prepared Corn on the Cob was resultingly and irreversibly soaked in honey and butter. When his temper settled and Rabbit begrudgingly tasted the dish . . . he was startled to discover a taste even more thrilling than Just So vegetables. (If such a thing can be believed.)

Remind dear Rabbit of that chapter when you cook him this—sweetcorn lathered in a dizzying blend of creamy butter and bright honey—with the added fermented saltiness of miso.

YIELD: 4 servings

- 113 grams (1 stick) unsalted butter, at room temperature
- 45 to 60 grams white miso
- 60 grams honey
- 4 ears corn on the cob, shucked

SPECIAL TOOLS
Electric whisk
Steamer insert or basket

NOTE: *Miso is a salty, savoury paste of fermented soybeans used in Japanese cuisine. The saltiness varies depending on the colour and brand, so adjust to taste.*

Use Up the Butter!

This recipe makes more whipped butter than you need for four ears of corn on the cob. Use leftovers to slather on crusty bread and scones or toss with steamed, grilled, or roasted vegetables.

In a medium bowl, use an electric whisk on low speed to beat the butter, 45 grams of miso, and the honey until combined. Taste and add more miso if you want it saltier. Increase the speed to high and whip until the butter is light and fluffy, about 3 minutes. Transfer to ramekins or small bowls and set aside.

Corn on the cob can be boiled or steamed, but steaming preserves more nutrients. Place a steamer insert or basket inside a pot large enough to hold the sweetcorn. Add enough water to come just below the bottom of the insert. Cover and bring the water to the boil over a high heat. Add the corn, cover, and let it steam until the kernels are bright and glossy and cooked through, 6 to 8 minutes.

Transfer the corn on the cob to a platter and serve with the honey-miso butter.

Walnut Baklava

When honey is needed for a recipe, one clever little game to keep Pooh (or any other sticky-fingered animals) from simply eating it all is to get him talking. A flowing stream of questions can keep the bear's thoughts drifting and swimming away from the amber sweetness waiting its turn in the mix.

If you were to make this Walnut Baklava, for example, good questions could include 'Have you ever been to the Mediterranean or Middle East, where this flaky, sweet pastry abounds?' or 'Do you like walnuts? Or should we use your favourite type of nut instead?' or 'When the crispy thin layers of filo dough crackle like fallen leaves, what autumn memories come to mind?'

Hopefully, by the end of your endeavour, sufficient amounts of honey remain to sweeten the cinnamon, cloves, and butter that round out this delicately delectable treat. And, perhaps, you will have grown in your friendship and knowledge of the little bear (or other baking companion).

YIELD: One 23-by-33-centimetre baklava

HONEY SYRUP
- 4 strips lemon peel
- 200 grams sugar
- 240 millilitres water
- 240 grams honey
- 30 millilitres freshly squeezed lemon juice
- 1 cinnamon stick
- Pinch kosher (coarse) salt

BAKLAVA
- 450 grams walnuts, toasted (see Ingredients and Methods, page 168)
- 25 grams sugar
- 7 grams ground cinnamon
- 1 gram ground cloves
- 1.65 grams kosher (coarse) salt
- One 450-gram package filo dough, thawed
- 282 grams (2½ sticks) unsalted butter, melted

NOTE: *Filo dough (aka phyllo or phyllo pastry) is unleavened dough rolled into paper-thin sheets. Look for it in the frozen section of your supermarket. Follow the package directions for thawing, usually overnight in the fridge. Be sure the dough is at room temperature before using.*

SPECIAL TOOLS
Food processor
Pastry brush

To make the honey syrup: In a small saucepan, combine the lemon peel, sugar, water, honey, lemon juice, cinnamon stick, and salt. Bring to the boil over a high heat. Reduce the heat to maintain a simmer and cook, stirring occasionally, for 5 minutes until the sugar dissolves and the mixture thickens slightly. Remove the pan from the heat and transfer the syrup to a heat-safe container. Set aside to cool. Once cooled, discard the peel and cinnamon stick and refrigerate the syrup.

To make the baklava: Preheat the oven to 180°C, or gas mark 4.

In a food processor, combine the walnuts, sugar, ground cinnamon, cloves, and salt. Pulse until the nuts are ground into a mix of sandy and pebbly nuts. Don't grind it too finely or the mixture will become a paste. Transfer the mixture to a bowl and set aside.

To keep the filo from drying out, gently unroll the filo. Filo sheet sizes may differ depending on

What Is Baklava?

Baklava is a crispy, flaky layered dessert of filo dough and chopped nuts soaked with a sweet syrup popular in the Mediterranean and Middle East. The Greek version usually includes walnuts, cinnamon, and a honey-sugar syrup. Other versions include pistachios, almonds, a mix of nuts, and a sugar-based simple syrup and are flavoured with orange blossom or rose water.

Winnie the Pooh's Morning Stoutness Exercises

This daily routine helps Pooh Bear maintain the shape he is comfortable with and works up his morning appetite.

- Arm stretches and turns
- (Attempted) toe touches
- Up-downs
- A march to the cupboard

the brand. If necessary, trim the sheets to fit the tin. Place the stack of unwrapped filo on a baking paper–lined baking tray. Cover the filo with a sheet of clingfilm, then top with a slightly damp tea towel.

Butter the bottom and sides of a 23-by-33-centimetre pan. Lay two sheets of filo in the prepared tin. To help avoid ripping the delicate sheets when buttering, drizzle butter over the sheet by dipping a pastry brush into the melted butter and letting the butter drip off over the filo. Then lightly brush to spread it. Be sure to brush the edges of the filo. Repeat layering three more times for a total of four sets of two layers of filo stacked in the pan. Sprinkle 30 to 40 grams of the nut mixture evenly over the buttered filo. It will be a very thin layer of nuts and will not cover the filo completely. Top with two sheets of filo and butter again. Repeat layering the filo, butter, and nut mixture until you have six sheets of filo remaining. (If your package of filo comes with two rolls, remember to use both rolls.) Lay down two sheets of filo and then butter. Repeat with the remaining four sheets of filo.

Using a very sharp knife, cut the baklava lengthways into four rows. Be sure to cut all the way through the filo to the bottom of the tin. Then cut the baklava diagonally to form seven or eight rows of diamonds. Drizzle with any remaining butter.

Bake the baklava until the filo is golden brown and crisp, about 45 minutes, rotating the tin halfway through. Remove the tin from the oven and immediately spoon the chilled syrup evenly over the baklava, making sure to get into the edges and grooves between the rows. (The cold syrup over the hot baklava helps keep the filo from getting soggy.) Let the baklava cool completely, preferably uncovered overnight to allow the syrup to distribute evenly.

Honey Apple Cupcakes with Honey Soft Cream Cheese Frosting

Of course, we must not forget Tigger. Though he will be the first to remind you that 'tiggers don't like honey,' they also don't like being left out of the fun. The simple solution lies in that tiggers love being Recognised. So even if he won't eat them, any Tigger you find would be proud to have these cupcakes enjoyed in his honour.

A fitting tribute, these Honey Apple Cupcakes are just as bursting with personality. The sweet and springy cake is excitingly spiced with cinnamon, ginger, nutmeg, and cloves. Topped with honey soft cream cheese frosting, they become a delectable treat (almost) as joyful and special as Tigger himself.

YIELD: 12 cupcakes

HONEY APPLE CUPCAKES
180 grams plain flour
6.9 grams baking powder
1.15 grams bicarbonate of soda
2.3 grams ground cinnamon
0.9 gram ground ginger
0.6 gram ground nutmeg
0.5 gram ground cloves
0.8 gram kosher (coarse) salt
113 grams (1 stick) unsalted butter, at room temperature
100 grams caster sugar
1 large egg, at room temperature
60 grams honey
2.5 millilitres vanilla essence
160 millilitres milk
1 crisp apple, peeled, cored, and grated

HONEY SOFT CREAM CHEESE FROSTING
Two 225-gram packages soft cream cheese, at room temperature
224 grams icing sugar
60 grams honey
Garnish Ideas: Store-bought edible honeybee decorations, Chocolate-Dipped Honeycomb Sweets (page 17), Chocolate Honeycomb Shards (recipe follows), dried apple slices, or candied ginger

SPECIAL TOOLS
Stand mixer
Piping bag
Small offset spatula

To make the honey apple cupcakes: Preheat the oven to 180°C, or gas mark 4. Line a standard muffin tin with cupcake liners.

In a medium bowl, whisk together the flour, baking powder, bicarbonate of soda, cinnamon, ginger, nutmeg, cloves, and salt.

In the bowl of a stand mixer fitted with a paddle attachment, cream the butter and caster sugar on medium-high speed until light and fluffy, 2 to 3 minutes. Scrape down the sides, add the egg, and mix until well blended. Add the honey and vanilla and mix on low speed just to combine.

Continued on page 34.

Alternate adding the dry ingredients and the milk to the creamed butter in three stages just until mixed. Give the grated apples a squeeze over the sink and then fold them into the batter.

Divide the batter evenly into the liners. Bake, rotating the tin halfway through, until a toothpick inserted in the middle of a cupcake comes out clean, about 20 minutes. Cool the cupcakes in the tin on a wire rack for 10 minutes. Then remove the cupcakes to the wire rack and cool completely.

To make the honey soft cream cheese frosting: In the bowl of a stand mixer fitted with the paddle attachment, beat the soft cream cheese on medium-high speed until soft and fluffy, about 1 minute. Scrape the sides and add the icing sugar. Beat on low speed just until mixed, then beat on medium-high speed until fluffy, about another minute. Add the honey and beat on low speed just until incorporated.

Pipe, swirl, or spread about 66 grams of the frosting per cupcake. Garnish as desired.

Chocolate Honeycomb Shards:
Melt 60 grams of chopped plain chocolate in a small microwave-safe bowl in 15-second intervals at 50 per cent power in the microwave. Once nearly melted, stir in 5 millilitres of neutral oil until smooth. Evenly spread the chocolate over a piece of clean and dry bubble wrap (about 25 by 10 centimetres) with small bubbles. You don't want it too thick but not too thin either. Let it harden, sticking it in the fridge if necessary. Peel off the hardened chocolate and break into smaller honeycomb shards to top the cupcakes.

Honey-Poached Pears

The young boy named Christopher Robin loved Winnie the Pooh so dearly that, even when they were apart, small things would turn his mind to the bear so completely that Christopher Robin would be surprised to remember Pooh was, in fact, elsewhere.

This was the case with Honey-Poached Pears. The first time Christopher Robin had been offered them, he was certain he had heard 'Honey-Poached *Bears*.' Though it was natural to think of Pooh upon hearing anything about honey, the thought of his beloved bear being Poached (or anywhere near Poachers) left Christopher Robin in terrible worry.

Thankfully, the various grown-ups around quickly repeated that the word had been *Pears* and shared with the young boy these deliciously prepared fruits. Though Pooh would likely prefer it with less pear and far more honey, Christopher Robin was delighted and soothed by the festive seasonings of cinnamon, ginger, and lemon dancing through the sweetness of honey, juicy ripe pear, and the whipped cream (with which it was served).

In the end, despite his initial fright, Christopher Robin thought this treat was a lovely way to be reminded of his friend Pooh.

YIELD: 4 servings

- 15 millilitres freshly squeezed lemon juice
- 4 Anjou pears, ripe but firm
- 1.2 litres water
- 3 coins ginger (no need to peel)
- 3 strips lemon peel
- 5 cardamom pods
- 1 cinnamon stick
- 107 grams honey
- Fresh mint leaves, for garnish
- Vanilla ice cream or whipped cream, for serving (optional)

Fill a large bowl about halfway with water and stir in the lemon juice.

Peel the pears, leaving the stems intact, cut a thin slice away from the bottom so they can stand upright, and put them into the acidulated water as you go to prevent them browning.

In a pan large enough to snugly hold all the pears, bring the water, ginger, lemon peel, cardamom, cinnamon, and honey to a simmer over a high heat. Using a slotted spoon, lower the pears into the water, turning them to coat in the liquid. Return to a simmer and cook until the pears are soft but firm and the tip of a paring knife easily pierces the flesh, 25 to 45 minutes, depending on the firmness of the pears. Turn the pears every so often during cooking to get the flavoured liquid into the flesh.

Transfer the pears to a bowl and cover to keep warm. (Alternatively, you can chill the pears and serve cold.) Simmer the liquid until it reduces by half, about 40 minutes.

Place the pears on plates and drizzle with the spiced syrup. Garnish with mint leaves and serve with ice cream or whipped cream if desired.

Honey Lemonade with Mint Ice Cubes

Of all Winnie the Pooh's friends, it is sometimes most difficult to see eye-to-eye with Eeyore. Usually, because the gloomy donkey is looking down—both literally and 'in a manner of speaking.' But after many unsuccessful attempts to brighten one of Eeyore's dour moods, Pooh has come to appreciate that being a friend does not always mean making someone happy. Sometimes it simply means being there. Very often, sharing a moment together where happiness and sadness sit comfortably side by side is all the comfort his friend needs.

The same such balance is struck in each glass of this Honey Lemonade. The soured tones of fresh lemon juice are brightened by the sweetness of honey. The minty ice cubes unfurl and share their flavour. And in the end, both sides are made all the richer for being together.

YIELD: 8 servings (about 1.9 litres)

Small fresh mint leaves, for filling the ice cube trays
480 grams honey
180 millilitres hot water
475 millilitres freshly squeezed lemon juice (from about 12 large, juicy lemons)
1.1 litres cold water

Fill standard ice cube trays with water. Place a small mint leaf in each cube compartment, leaving some of the leaf sticking out of the water. Transfer to the freezer and freeze until solid.

NOTE: *If you have large cocktail ice cube trays, you could use those instead and float a mint leaf on top.*

In a medium microwave-safe bowl or large liquid measuring cup, microwave the honey and hot water in 10-second bursts. You just want it to flow a little more easily for mixing and pouring but not make it too hot. Stir to combine. Let cool.

In a 1.9-litre pitcher or larger, combine the lemon juice and honey water. Add the cold water and stir. Pour into glasses and add mint ice cubes to serve.

Chapter 2

Parties and Picnics

The days when Christopher Robin came round to play were always ones of great excitement.

Winnie the Pooh, of course, was ever glad to see his friend. But Piglet, and Eeyore, and Rabbit, and Kanga and Roo (and Tigger, too) were so quick to turn their plans and attention to the visiting boy that the Wood practically became a party, simply through such gathering and enthusiasm.

With these festive gatherings (and the usual need for snacks and refreshments) happening so joyously often, the residents of the Hundred-Acre Wood soon became quite expert at preparing various dishes, desserts, and delights to be shared amongst friends.

Here, then, is an assortment of recipes to populate your next party or picnic. With the flavours and excitement they bring, it may feel just like Christopher Robin and all his friends are bounding their way to join you.

Hero Cake

If one is lucky enough to have Very Good Friends, one will likely have occasion to celebrate their doing a Very Brave or Very Kind thing. An example of both such occasions being when Winnie the Pooh bravely and kindly rescued his good friend Piglet from a terrible flood. (At least, it is the example Pooh most often brings up himself.) Such goodness deserves to be celebrated, and celebrations, of course, deserve a cake.

This Hero Cake serves as a perfect token of appreciation or centrepiece to larger festivities. Classic and crowd-pleasing sweet cocoa-buttercream frosting drapes two layers of fluffy cake. The zestiness of raspberries blended into the cake and a middle layer of raspberry preserves add their own energetic 'Hip-hip-hurray!' to the proceedings. (Though, the freeze-dried berries may give the cake a greyish cast. So a bit of red food colouring may create a more appropriately joyous look.) Finally, decorative touches of pure buttercream properly signify this is a Very Special cake for a Very Special person. (And never hesitate to consider the Very Special person deserving such recognition may be *you*.)

YIELD: One 2-layer 23-centimetre cake

CAKE
- 169 grams (1½ sticks) unsalted butter, at room temperature, plus more for greasing the tin
- 330 grams sifted soft-wheat flour or plain flour, plus more for dusting the tins
- One 37-gram package freeze-dried raspberries
- 300 grams caster sugar
- 18.4 grams baking powder
- 1.65 grams kosher (coarse) salt
- 240 millilitres milk, at room temperature, divided
- Red gel food colour, as needed (optional)
- 5 large egg whites, at room temperature
- 10 millilitres vanilla essence

FROSTING
- 450 grams unsalted butter, at room temperature
- 392 grams icing sugar, divided
- 120 to 180 millilitres milk, at room temperature, divided
- 15 millilitres vanilla essence
- 1.65 grams kosher (coarse) salt
- Orange (or red and yellow) gel food colour, as needed
- 80 grams Dutch-process cocoa powder

ASSEMBLY
- 60 grams raspberry preserves

SPECIAL TOOLS
Food processor
Stand mixer
Offset spatula
Cake pedestal (optional)

To make the cake: Preheat the oven to 180°C, or gas mark 4. Butter two 23-centimetre round cake tins and line the bottoms with baking paper. Butter again and dust lightly with flour. Set aside.

In a food processor, grind the raspberries into a powder. Sift through a fine-mesh sieve (to remove the seeds) into the bowl of a stand mixer fitted with the paddle attachment. Discard the seeds. Add the flour, caster sugar, baking powder, and salt to the bowl and mix on low speed to combine. Add the butter, 180 millilitres of milk, and some red food colour (if using). Mix on low speed to combine. Increase the speed to medium and continue to beat for 1½ minutes, scraping down the sides of the bowl halfway through.

In a medium bowl or 475-millilitre liquid measuring

Continued on page 44.

Parties and Picnics 43

cup, lightly whisk the remaining 60 millilitres of milk, the egg whites, and vanilla. Add one-third of the egg mixture (you can eyeball it) to the batter and beat on medium speed for 20 seconds. Scrape down the sides of the bowl. Add half of the remaining egg mixture, beat for 20 seconds, and scrape down the sides of the bowl. Add the remaining egg mixture, beat for 20 seconds, and scrape down the sides of the bowl. Divide the batter evenly between the prepared cake tins and smooth the tops. Bake until a tester comes out clean and the tops spring back when lightly pressed, about 25 minutes. The cakes will be slightly domed but will flatten as they cool. Let the cakes cool in the tins for 10 minutes. If necessary, run a knife between the cakes and sides of the tins to loosen. Invert the cakes onto a cooling rack and gently peel off the baking paper. Let the cakes cool completely.

To make the frosting: In the bowl of a stand mixer fitted with a paddle attachment, beat the butter on medium speed until light and fluffy, about 3 minutes. Add 112 grams of icing sugar, 60 millilitres of milk, the vanilla, and salt and beat another minute. Decrease the speed to low and gradually add the remaining 280 grams of icing sugar, 56 grams at a time, until incorporated. Increase the speed to medium-high and beat another minute, scraping down the sides of the bowl, until smooth.

Put 108 grams of the frosting into a medium bowl and add the orange (or a mix of red and yellow) food colour. Whisk until smooth, adding more colour until you obtain the shade of orange desired. Transfer to a piping bag or sandwich-size zip-top bag. If using a zip-top bag, push the filling to one of the bottom corners of the bag. Snip off the corner when ready to frost.

To the remaining plain frosting in the mixer bowl, add the cocoa powder and another 60 millilitres of milk and beat on medium speed until smooth. If the frosting is too thick, add more milk, 15 millilitres at a time, to thin it out.

To assemble the cake: If the cake tops haven't flattened enough, use a long serrated knife to level the tops. Place a cake layer top side up on a flat surface. With one hand, hold the knife blade flat against the lowest part of the dome. Place your other hand lightly on the top of the dome. Slowly and carefully saw back and forth with the knife until you get to the other side of the dome, using the edge of the cake as a guide to get an even trim. (Remove the dome and save it to nibble on.) Repeat with the other cake layer if necessary.

Place a cake layer bottom side up on a flat plate or cake pedestal. Use an offset spatula to spread about 160 grams of the frosting over the top. Spread raspberry preserves over the frosting. Top with the other cake layer bottom side up. Spread the remaining chocolate frosting over the top and sides of the cake. Squeeze dots of orange frosting over the top and sides of the cake.

Dirt Cake Trifle

Though Rabbit prefers his vegetables (and a degree of order and calm rarely found at parties), he can easily be won over and put aside any grumbling when friends play a bit to his interests. To wit, Kanga once quickly and cleverly revised a somewhat traditional English trifle into a dessert after Rabbit's own heart.

Restrained in its sweetness but ripe with delight, this layered dessert plants tiers of soft pound cake, fresh strawberries, tangy lemon curd, and whipped cream. The top cultivates a garden aesthetic of crushed graham crackers for the ground and dipped strawberries to make plump little carrots that will make any rabbit want to dig in.

YIELD: 10 to 12 servings

'CARROTS'
- 85 grams white candy melts (see Ingredients and Methods, page 168)
- 30 millilitres neutral oil
- Orange (or red and yellow) gel food colour, as needed
- 8 small strawberries with nice green leaves, at room temperature (see Note at right)

TRIFLE
- 340 grams pound cake, sliced 12 millimetres thick (about 11 slices), divided
- About 560 grams lemon curd, divided (see Ingredients and Methods, page 168)
- About 14 large strawberries, hulled and sliced 6 millimetres thick, divided
- 240 millilitres double cream, whipped to firm peaks, divided (see Ingredients and Methods, page 168)
- 9 chocolate graham crackers, finely crushed

SPECIAL TOOLS
- 2.4-litre glass bowl or trifle bowl
- Food processor
- Electric whisk
- Small offset spatula

To make the 'carrots': In a coffee mug (for easier dipping), melt the candy melts according to package directions. Stir in the oil and then add food colour, a drop at a time, until it's a colour you like for carrots. If the melts start to get hard, microwave for a few seconds at a time to loosen. Poke a fork through the stem end of a small strawberry and then dip and turn it in the candy melts to coat. (You can also use a small offset spatula or rubber spatula to help coat.) Place the strawberries on a silicone mat or baking paper to harden.

NOTE: *If the strawberries you use for the carrots are too cold, the candy melts will harden immediately and make it difficult to get a smooth coating.*

To make the trifle: In a 2.4-litre glass bowl, line the bottom with two slices of pound cake, cutting as needed to fill in the spaces. Spread about 160 grams of the lemon curd over the cake. Scatter some sliced strawberries over the curd, arranging some against the sides of the bowl for a nicer display. Spread about 60 grams of the whipped cream over the strawberries. For the second layer, use about three slices of pound cake, 160 grams of lemon curd, a little more strawberries, and about 90 grams of whipped cream. For the third layer, use about six slices of pound cake, 240 grams of lemon curd, and the remaining strawberries and whipped cream. Scatter the graham cracker crumbs over top for the 'dirt.' Place the 'carrots' in rows snuggled into the dirt.

Parties and Picnics

Rabbit

'What a refreshing day for harvesting.'

Devoted as Rabbit is to his garden, he's even more devoted to his friends. (Even when he seems frustrated.) Rabbit is always happy to share his home-grown goodness with Pooh and the rest, but surprising him with a vegetarian dish of your own can cheer him out of a cranky mood. In addition to the recipes throughout chapter 3 (pages 71–93), which are inspired by the delicious produce Rabbit grows, you can find a handful of Rabbit-inspired recipes throughout the book.

RECIPES:

Corn on the Cob with Whipped Honey-Miso Butter . . . . page 29

Dirt Cake Trifle. . . . . page 47

Roasted Vegetable Platter with Honey Butter Glaze. . . . page 119

Asparagus, Potato, and Pecorino Frittata . . . . page 129

Za'atar Roasted Chickpeas, Butternut Squash, and Red Onions with Lime Yoghurt . . page 133

Fresh Cabbage Pancakes. . . . page 150

Pooh's Pasties . . . . page 153

Kiwi and Strawberry Ice Lollies. . . . . page 165

Thumbprint Biscuits

On rainy days in the Hundred-Acre Wood, Winnie the Pooh and his friends are still happy to have a party. Though, preferably, out of the rain. And one that does not require much coming-and-going to get special things needed for the usual sorts of parties. One particularly successful idea, then, was Kanga's suggestion of a Baking Party.

These simple (ingredient-wise, at least) and classic Thumbprint Biscuits can be made with ingredients likely hiding in the pantry. And with many helping hands (or paws, as it were), the pressing and filling of so many biscuits can be a quick and together-ish bit of fun. When finished, these buttery bites dusted with excitements of sugar and pops of bright jam are perfect little celebrations—or pair nicely with a warming cup of tea as you wait for the rain to pass.

YIELD: About 35 biscuits

160 grams red jam
183 grams sugar, divided
226 grams (2 sticks) unsalted butter, at room temperature
1.65 grams kosher (coarse) salt
15 millilitres vanilla essence
270 grams plain flour, sifted

SPECIAL TOOLS
Stand mixer
Round 2.5-millilitre measuring spoon (optional)

Preheat the oven to 190°C, or gas mark 5. Line two baking trays with baking paper and set them aside. In a small bowl, stir the jam to break up any lumps. In a separate small bowl, put 50 grams of sugar. Set the bowls aside.

In the bowl of a stand mixer fitted with the paddle attachment, beat the remaining 133 grams of sugar, the butter, and salt on medium-high speed until pale yellow and fluffy, about 4 minutes. Scrape down the sides of the bowl. Add the vanilla and beat until combined. Scrape down the bowl. With the motor running on low speed, add the flour to the butter mixture, 30 grams at a time, scraping down the bowl as needed, until a soft, pliable dough forms.

Scoop about 15 grams of dough and roll it between your palms to form a smooth 3-centimetre ball. Roll the ball in the bowl of reserved sugar to coat it and transfer it to a prepared baking tray. Gently press the back of a round 2.5-millilitre measuring spoon (or your thumb, but it won't be as smooth or consistent) into the top of the ball to form a

Continued on page 50.

Parties and Picnics 49

round indentation. Don't worry if the ball forms small cracks on its sides—just use your finger to smooth them out. Repeat with the remaining dough, dividing the biscuits between the two trays, allowing at least 4 centimetres between the biscuits. Fill each indentation with enough jam to sit slightly above the rim of the indentation. Bake, rotating the trays halfway through, until the biscuits' bottom edges are lightly golden, 14 to 16 minutes. Cool the biscuits on the baking trays.

Tips for Success

- The shortbread biscuits served at the Hero Party had a red filling, but any jam colour will be pretty.
- This is a great way to use up those almost-empty jars of jam in the fridge.
- If you prefer not to roll the balls in sugar, dip the back of the measuring spoon in sugar before forming the indentations to prevent the spoon sticking to the dough.

Open-Faced Radish and Herbed Cheese Tea Sandwiches

If not for Christopher Robin, Pooh thought, he would know so little about the world outside of the Hundred-Acre Wood. That in something called 'Polite Society,' grown-ups must discuss the weather or ask each other about their 'weak end.' Or, that 'proper' parties (the kind without tree climbing) must always include small sandwiches with spreads and some vegetables. This simple teatime (or other polite gathering) sandwich accents creamy, herbed cheese with light strips of the sharp, peppery flavour of radish on the deeper, earthier tones of pumpernickel bread.

YIELD: 10 tea sandwiches

10 slices pumpernickel sandwich bread

NOTE: *Feel free to use the cocktail-size pumpernickel bread if you can find it.*

One 150.25-gram round herbed soft cheese spread, at room temperature

About 5 radishes, thinly sliced

Flaky sea salt

Microgreens and fresh herbs, for garnish (optional)

Cut the bread into rectangles about 5 by 10 centimetres. (Use crusts to make croutons or breadcrumbs.) Spread each with about 15 grams of soft cheese spread. Layer the sliced radishes over top. Sprinkle a few granules of flaky sea salt on top. Garnish with microgreens and fresh herbs if desired.

Picnic Planning

No one really needs an excuse to enjoy a picnic with friends and relations. But perhaps planning one may be all the more exciting when it is for a special occasion.

Hero Party: Throw a surprise picnic in someone's honour as a special thank-you to fill their heart and tummy.

Stargazing: A dinner picnic can set you in a perfect place for taking in constellations or special celestial events.

Explorer's Reward: Don't settle for snacks on your next adventure. Pack a full picnic to celebrate your new discoveries!

Cucumber, Dill, and Avocado Pressed Rice Sandwiches

Another perfectly lovely option for the Proper Party sandwich assortment, this recipe adds an element of worldly exploration. Though crisp, refreshing cucumber and bright, herbaceous dill are familiar friends amongst tea sandwiches, the additions of avocado as a creamy spread and sushi-style rice in place of bread set off in a more adventurous direction around the globe. Perhaps ideal for celebrating Pooh's discovering the North Pole, or to pack for an expedition to find the East and West ones.

YIELD: 32 bite-size sandwiches

350 grams uncooked short- or medium-grain sushi rice

350 millilitres water

45 millilitres unseasoned rice vinegar

37.5 grams sugar

5 grams kosher (coarse) salt

½ cucumber (about 15 centimetres long)

16 grams chopped fresh dill, plus sprigs for garnish

1 medium avocado, ripe but firm, cut lengthways into 3-millimetre-thick slices

8 millilitres freshly squeezed lemon juice

SPECIAL TOOLS

Large fine-mesh sieve

One 20-by-20-centimetre baking pan

Mandoline slicer (optional)

Pastry brush

Something flat that fits into the baking tin to press the rice evenly (see Tips for Success)

Sharp knife with a thin blade

In a medium saucepan with a tight-fitting lid, combine the rice and enough water to cover. Using your fingers, gently swish the rice around in a circle until the water gets cloudy. Drain in a large fine-mesh sieve. Repeat two more times, then return the rice to the pan. Add the water to the pan and smooth the surface of the rice. Bring it to the boil, then cover and reduce the heat to medium-low. Cook until the moisture is absorbed, about 15 minutes. Let it sit, covered, for 5 to 10 minutes.

Meanwhile, in a small saucepan, combine the vinegar, sugar, and salt. Bring to a simmer over a medium heat, stirring to dissolve the sugar and salt. Set aside.

Gently spread the rice over the bottom and partially up the sides of a large mixing bowl. Sprinkle the vinegar mixture all over the rice. Mix gently but thoroughly, making sure not to smash the rice. The rice may seem wet, but don't worry—it will dry as it sits and absorbs the vinegar mixture. Let the rice cool enough to handle but still be warm, 10 to 15 minutes.

While the rice is cooling, line a 20-by-20-centimetre baking tin with two crossing sheets of clingfilm, allowing a generous excess (13 to 15 centimetres on each side) to drape over the sides of the pan.

Continued on page 56.

Parties and Picnics 55

Press the clingfilm into the edges and corners of the tin. Set aside.

Using a vegetable peeler, peel the cucumber skin lengthways in stripes, allowing the skin of half the cucumber to remain. Using a mandoline or sharp knife, slice the cucumber into 2-millimetre-thin rounds. Line the prepared tin in rows of slightly overlapping (like roof shingles) cucumber slices. Wet your hands with water so the rice doesn't stick to them. Spread half of the rice in a thin layer over the cucumbers and press down firmly. Sprinkle the dill over the rice. Arrange the avocado slices in a single layer over the dill and brush with the lemon juice to keep it from discolouring. Wet your hands again and spread the remaining rice over the avocados. Press down firmly.

Fold the excess ends of clingfilm over the rice to cover it completely. Use something flat that fits inside of the baking tin to press down on the rice evenly and very, very firmly so the layers stick together; otherwise, it will fall apart when you cut it. Using your body weight, press all over, going over the surface several times. Be sure to press the edges and corners, too.

Unwrap the rice and invert it onto a chopping board so the cucumber side is facing up. Use a sharp knife with a thin blade. Dampen the blade so the rice doesn't stick to it. Cut the pressed rice into 16 squares. Then cut each square into two triangles. Cover with a sheet of clingfilm until ready to serve. Garnish each sandwich with dill before serving.

Tips for Success

- These cucumber sandwiches are based on Japanese pressed sushi called *oshizushi*, which uses a special wooden or plastic mould. In this recipe, to compress the rice, use something flat that fits into the baking tin to press the rice evenly, like the bottom of a sturdy square or rectangular food storage container. In a pinch, a wide, metal offset turner or the bottom of a metal measuring cup will work.

- When choosing your rice, look for Japanese-style short- and medium-grain white rice, often labeled sushi rice. Avoid Italian and Spanish short- and medium-grain rice such as Arborio, Carnaroli, and bomba, which are used for risotto and paella.

- Do not refrigerate the pressed rice or the rice will harden.

Piglet

'It's hard to be brave when you're a very small animal.'

Our dear little Piglet is, in fact, a creature possessing enormous heart and equally tremendous worry. It is the comfort of his friends that gives him confidence and courage. So, to share a bit of comfort food, consider the following Piglet-friendly dishes.

RECIPES:

Honey Nut Granola . . . . page 25

Haycorn Tea . . . . page 59

Smoked Paprika Baked
Acorn Squash . . . . page 86

Sweetcorn and
Potato Chowder . . . . page 134

Piglet's Big Goat's
Cheese Log. . . . . page 145

Haycorns . . . . page 158

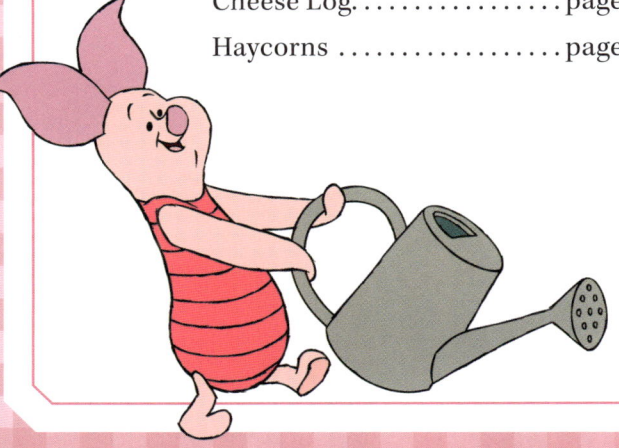

Haycorn Tea

Lest we forget our smaller guests at celebrations and teatimes (be it dear Piglet or other diminutive loved ones), this roasted barley 'tea' offers a tasty and non-caffeinated alternative. Piglet, of course, is already quite jittery. Instead, the toasty, nutty flavour evokes Piglet's favourite haycorn flavours in each delightful sip.

YIELD: 4 servings (about 1.2 litres)

50 grams pearl barley
1.4 litres water

> **Exploring Roasted Barley**
>
> Roasted barley tea is an unsweetened caffeine-free beverage that's very popular amongst children in some East Asian countries (particularly Korea and Japan). It's especially refreshing served over ice on a hot day.
>
> Once strained, the spent barley can be tossed into a salad, grain bowl, or soup. It's quite tasty mixed with any leftover slow-roasted tomatoes from the Tomato and Herbed Ricotta Galette (page 83).

In a small frying pan over medium heat, toast the barley, stirring occasionally, until it begins to take on some colour and smell nutty, about 5 minutes. Reduce the heat to medium-low and continue to toast until the kernels are dark brown, about another 20 minutes.

In a medium saucepan, combine the roasted barley and water and bring to the boil. Reduce the heat to maintain a simmer, then simmer for 10 minutes. If drinking the tea hot, strain the tea through a fine-mesh sieve, divide amongst four cups, and serve. If serving cold, strain the tea into a metal bowl and cool in an ice bath. Transfer to a pitcher and chill in the refrigerator. Serve over ice.

Coronation Chicken Sliders

Amongst all this talk of sandwiches, there came a slight rumbling.

It grew louder and growlier, until Piglet (were he present) would certainly have worried aloud whether it might be a woozle or Heffalump. (Forgetting, in his worry, the differences of what each sounded like.)

One final roar shook loudly enough that it was immediately clear the rumble was, in fact, my own tummy. (An embarrassment, I assure you.) So I should pause this talk of parties and picnics to make myself the particular sandwich I had begun imagining (inspired by assorted ingredients on hand and not yet expired)—creamy, curry-seasoned chicken mixed with sparks of sweetness from apricots or sultanas and mango chutney on a warmed and fluffy sweet roll. (Or perhaps several such sandwiches, as there will be quite a bit more food still to discuss, and it would be terribly rude to keep interrupting.)

YIELD: 12 sliders

- One 150.25-gram container natural Greek yoghurt
- 160 grams mayonnaise
- 84 grams mango or Major Grey's chutney
- 16 grams finely chopped fresh chives
- 12.5 grams curry powder
- 15 millilitres Worcestershire sauce
- 9 grams kosher (coarse) salt
- Freshly ground black pepper
- 420 grams 6-millimetre-diced chicken (from a rotisserie chicken)
- 85 grams 6-millimetre-diced soft apricots (about 14 apricots) or sultanas
- One 340-gram package sweet dinner rolls

In a large bowl, combine the yoghurt, mayonnaise, chutney, chives, curry powder, Worcestershire sauce, salt, and pepper to taste. Mix well. Add the chicken and apricots and stir to coat. Adjust the seasonings as needed and set aside.

Using a serrated knife, cut the sheet of sweet dinner rolls in half horizontally without separating the rolls. If you'd like the rolls toasted, set an oven shelf to about 15 centimetres below the grill element and preheat the grill on high. Place the sheets of rolls cut side up on a baking tray. Toast under the grill until the bread is golden, 30 to 45 seconds. Watch carefully so that they don't burn. Spread the chicken mixture evenly on the bottom half of the rolls, then cover with the top half. Cut into individual sliders and serve.

Soaking Dried Fruit

Plump up hard, dried-out dried fruits by putting them in a heatproof bowl, covering them with boiling water, and then letting them soak for 10 to 15 minutes. Drain, dry, and let cool.

Smoked Trout Dip

A lovely thing about big gatherings is the occasion to see the special sort of people who (for one reason or another) are not quite part of your day-to-day. For Winnie the Pooh, one such friend is Owl. Though a good friend (to him, Christopher Robin, and the rest), the wise old bird prefers an afternoon of study when others play. (Owl is so learned, in fact, he has been witnessed even reading books upside down or back to front!)

So, to make a unique and specialised guest such as he feel fully welcome, consider including a dish catered to his tastes. This equally unique serving of a versatile cheese dip deepens its flavour with smoked trout (as any erudite bird would enjoy). Irresistibly seasoned with tarragon, lemon zest, and salty capers, the result is as fittingly sophisticated a spread as one could find in any book.

YIELD: About 525 grams

- 225 grams soft cream cheese, at room temperature
- 60 grams soured cream
- 4 grams chopped fresh tarragon leaves
- 9 grams drained capers, minced
- 2 grams freshly grated lemon zest
- 225 grams cold-smoked trout, skin removed if present
- Assorted savoury biscuits and crudités, for serving

In a large bowl, mix together the soft cream cheese, soured cream, tarragon, capers, and lemon zest. Break the trout into flakes. Gently fold the trout into the soft cream cheese dip. Serve with savoury biscuits and crudités.

Dip Tips
- If you have time, let the dip sit for 30 to 60 minutes to allow the flavours to bloom. Have no fear, for the dip is still delicious if time doesn't allow.
- The quick pickled onions (see page 90) make a great topper.

Parties and Picnics

Creamy Potato Salad with Pickled Mustard Seeds and Spring Onions

Whether party or picnic, gatherings are always improved by a rich variety of both guests and dishes. Popular and showy ones, curious and new ones, and, of course, reliable old familiars. Just as there are Comfort Foods, we enjoy Comfort Friends. Warm, simple, and unwavering, they seem to always be there for you, just as they were. This might equally describe a tried-and-true potato salad or the dependably dour Eeyore. With this creamy recipe in particular, it's just as hearty and mellow.

YIELD: 8 servings

PICKLED MUSTARD SEEDS
90 millilitres white wine vinegar
22 grams yellow mustard seeds
12.5 grams sugar
0.8 gram kosher (coarse) salt

POTATO SALAD
1.4 kilograms Yukon Gold or other yellow potatoes, scrubbed and cut into 2-centimetre chunks

NOTE: *Don't bother peeling the skins of Yukon Gold and other yellow potatoes—they're thin and tender enough to eat.*

15 grams kosher (coarse) salt, divided
Freshly ground black pepper
240 grams mayonnaise
67.5 grams thinly sliced spring onions (about 6 spring onions), divided

SPECIAL TOOL
Small fine-mesh sieve

To make the pickled mustard seeds: In a small saucepan, bring the vinegar, mustard seeds, sugar, and salt to the boil over high heat. Reduce the heat to maintain a very gentle simmer and cook for about 10 minutes, stirring once or twice to dissolve the sugar. Remove from the heat and set aside. The seeds will plump up as they sit.

To make the potato salad: Line a baking tray with foil and set aside.

In a large pot, combine the potatoes, 10 grams of salt, and enough water to cover by 2.5 centimetres. Bring to the boil over a high heat, then reduce the heat to maintain a simmer. Cook until the potatoes are cooked through, about 10 minutes.

In a large colander, drain the potatoes well. Spread the potatoes in an even layer on the prepared baking tray. Sprinkle the pickled mustard seeds (and their vinegar), the remaining 5 grams salt, and pepper to taste over the hot potatoes. Using a large spoon or rubber spatula, toss the potatoes gently. Let cool, about 30 minutes.

NOTE: *Spreading the potatoes on a baking tray allows for more even distribution when seasoning and is gentler than tossing in a bowl.*

Plop spoonfuls of mayo over the potatoes. Set aside 22.5 grams of spring onions for garnish. Scatter the remaining 45 grams of spring onions over the potatoes. Toss gently to coat. Taste and adjust the seasonings as needed. Transfer the potato salad to a serving bowl and sprinkle with the reserved spring onions.

Salted Watermelon Punch with Cucumber and Basil

In young Roo's opinion, it isn't a real party without a big bowl of punch, and a bright and festive centrepiece drink for all to enjoy certainly signals celebration. Fortunately for Kanga, this colourful and refreshing beverage can be made with a few simple items from the pantry and garden. The natural sweetness of watermelon juice is lightened with cucumber and given an extra hint of freshness through notes of basil.

YIELD: 4 to 6 servings (about 1.4 litres)

BASIL SIMPLE SYRUP
50 grams sugar
60 millilitres water
35 grams fresh basil leaves

WATERMELON PUNCH
1 cucumber
One 6.8-kilogram seedless watermelon
3.3 grams kosher (coarse) salt
Basil sprigs, for garnish

SPECIAL TOOL
Blender

Salting Fruit

Sprinkling salt on fruits like watermelon or cantaloupe is a popular practice in many parts of the world. It lessens any bitterness and increases the sweet flavour of the fruit.

To make the basil simple syrup: In a small saucepan, combine the sugar, water, and basil. Bring to a simmer over the medium-high heat and stir until the sugar dissolves, 1 to 2 minutes. Let cool with the basil in the syrup. Strain into a small bowl or jar, pressing on the basil to essence all the syrup (makes 80 millilitres).

To make the watermelon punch: Save about 2.5 centimetres of the cucumber for garnish. Peel the rest of the cucumber and cut into several large chunks. Put in a blender.

Cut the watermelon in half crosswise (so you have a deep bowl shape). Scoop out the watermelon flesh from one half and put it into the blender. Reserve the other half of the watermelon for another use. Blend the watermelon and cucumber until smooth. Strain the juice into a large bowl, discarding the pulp. Stir in the salt. Add the basil simple syrup 15 millilitres at a time until it tastes good to you (the amount will depend on the sweetness of the melon). If you have extra simple syrup, cover and store it in the refrigerator for up to two weeks. It's great for lemonade or sparkling water.

Pour the punch into the hollowed-out watermelon half. Thinly slice the reserved cucumber and float in the punch or use to garnish individual glasses. Ladle the punch into ice-filled glasses and garnish with basil sprigs.

Parties and Picnics

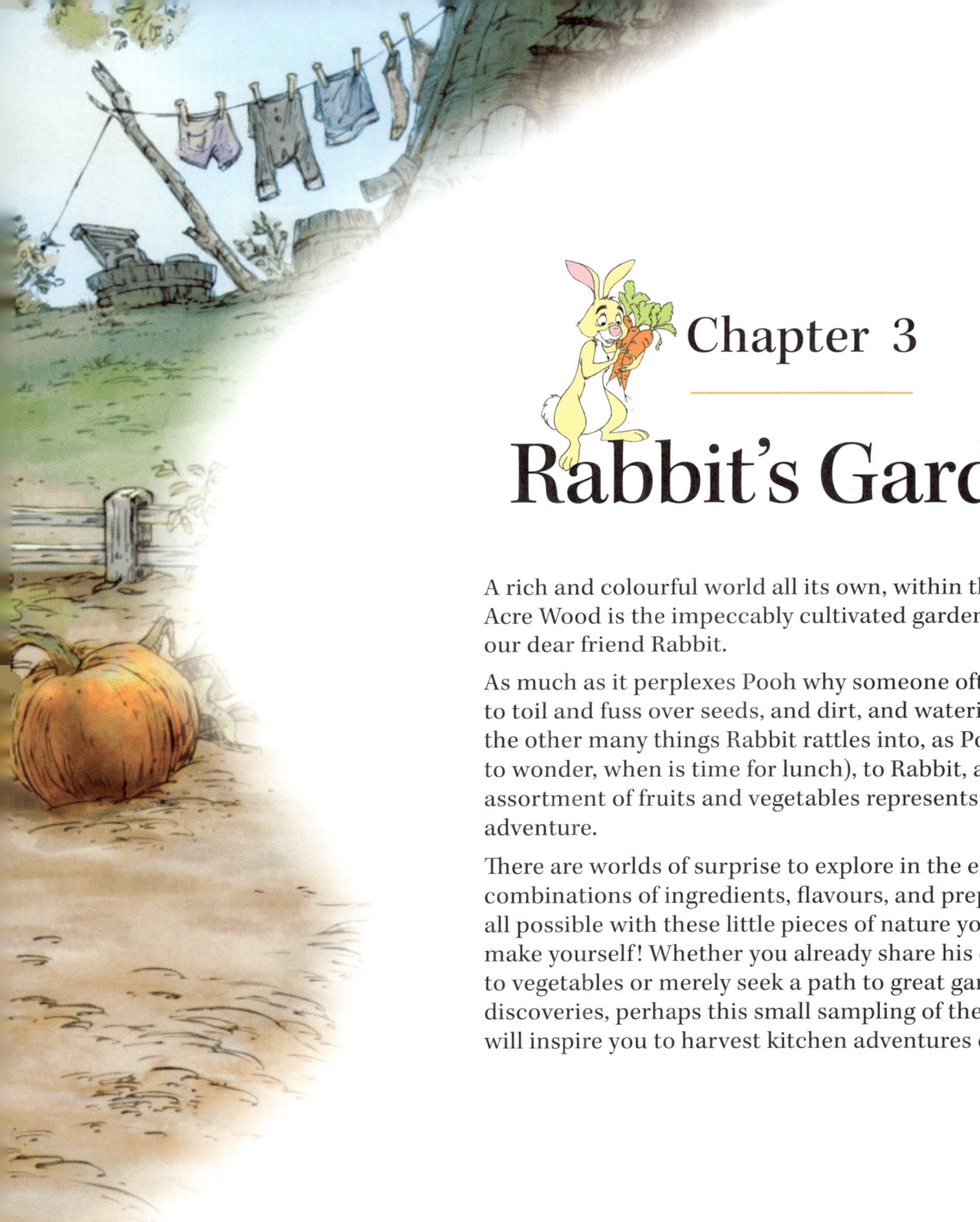

Chapter 3
Rabbit's Garden

A rich and colourful world all its own, within the Hundred-Acre Wood is the impeccably cultivated garden belonging our dear friend Rabbit.

As much as it perplexes Pooh why someone often chooses to toil and fuss over seeds, and dirt, and watering (and the other many things Rabbit rattles into, as Pooh begins to wonder, when is time for lunch), to Rabbit, a great assortment of fruits and vegetables represents its own adventure.

There are worlds of surprise to explore in the endless combinations of ingredients, flavours, and preparations—all possible with these little pieces of nature you can make yourself! Whether you already share his devotion to vegetables or merely seek a path to great garden discoveries, perhaps this small sampling of the possibilities will inspire you to harvest kitchen adventures of your own.

Wedge Salad with Carrot-Ginger Dressing

Though rabbits (small *r*, to be noted) are thought to love carrots, Rabbit (capital *R*) can attest that leafy greens are the cornerstone of meals for his kind. But on top of a cornerstone, so many wondrous things can be built. (Yes, Rabbit sees that carrots are notably present in many of those dishes, but that does not negate his argument!) In this case, a large base of crisp and refreshing lettuce is supported by bright and juicy cucumber and engulfed in a sweet and flavourful carrot purée enlivened with tastes of honey, miso, and ginger.

YIELD: 4 servings

NOTE: *This makes more dressing than you think you'll need, but you'll want to add more to the salad as you eat it.*

- 3 medium carrots, chopped
- 1 medium shallot, chopped
- One 7.5-by-2.5-centimetre knob fresh ginger, peeled and chopped
- 75 millilitres unseasoned rice vinegar
- 60 grams honey
- 30 grams white miso
- 30 millilitres water
- 10 millilitres toasted sesame oil (optional)
- 1.65 grams kosher (coarse) salt
- Freshly ground black pepper
- 60 millilitres neutral oil
- 1 medium head iceberg lettuce, quartered and cored (about 850 grams)
- 2 Persian cucumbers, halved lengthways and sliced crosswise
- Thinly sliced fresh chives, for garnish

SPECIAL TOOL
Blender

In a blender, combine the carrots, shallot, ginger, vinegar, honey, miso, water, sesame oil (if using), salt, and pepper to taste. Purée at low speed and increase to high speed as you go until the mixture is relatively smooth. Because of the raw carrots, this dressing won't get completely smooth. Transfer the mixture to a bowl and whisk in the neutral oil. (Processing the oil in the blender aerates the dressing and changes the texture.) Taste the dressing and adjust the seasonings as needed. Cover and refrigerate until ready to serve. The dressing will thicken as it sits, so if not using immediately, whisk in some water to thin as much as you like before serving.

Spoon some dressing on the centre of each of four salad plates. Arrange a lettuce wedge and some cucumbers on top of the dressing. Drizzle with more of the dressing and sprinkle with some chives. Serve the remaining dressing on the side.

Sugar Snap Peas, Watercress, and Mint Salad

A bit like Rabbit himself, baby watercress greens are both bright and somewhat peppery. No wonder they were used to round out the crisp sweetness of sugar snap peas in this particular garden expedition. For fuller flavour, the mix is drizzled with a sweet-and-tangy blend of honey, lemon, Dijon, and seasoning—with a brightening of mint.

YIELD: 4 servings

- 1 small shallot, finely diced
- 1 clove garlic, grated
- Zest and juice of 1 small lemon
- 15 millilitres extra-virgin olive oil
- 20 grams honey
- 10 grams Dijon mustard
- 1.65 grams kosher (coarse) salt
- Freshly ground black pepper
- 340 grams sugar snap peas
- 60 ounces baby watercress
- 10 grams fresh mint leaves, torn

NOTE: *Delicate, peppery baby watercress can be found packaged in bags with other salad greens. Baby rocket is a good substitute.*

In a small bowl, whisk together the shallot, garlic, lemon zest and juice, oil, honey, mustard, salt, and pepper to taste. Adjust the seasonings as you like.

Trim the sugar snap peas and thinly slice them on a diagonal. In a large bowl, toss the sugar snaps with the dressing. Add the watercress and mint and toss. Adjust the seasonings as needed and serve immediately.

Smashed Celery Salad with Grainy Mustard Dressing

If there is, in the world, an exact opposite to Rabbit's ordered, quiet garden, it may just be Tigger. His boundless bouncing, tussling, and tumbling are often not just a distraction to Rabbit's work, but a danger to the vegetables themselves. After a great many mishaps, frustrations, and catastrophes, Rabbit recognised he can no more change his friend's nature than he can grow a tomato into a swede. So he tried instead to put a purpose (and a particular place) to Tigger's energy when the (nonetheless) good friend would visit.

The work of this simple, light salad is largely in the smashing of celery. If you haven't got a Tigger on hand to bounce it into pieces, a mallet or similar tool may do. The tangy mustard and cider vinegar dressing (cut with a hint of sugar) is easily prepared for a salad that may be served quickly, to help set guests on their way.

YIELD: 4 servings

- 30 grams whole-grain mustard
- 10 grams Dijon mustard
- 15 millilitres apple cider vinegar
- 8.3 grams sugar
- 4 stalks celery, trimmed and patted dry
- 15 grams tender light green and yellow celery leaves

SPECIAL TOOLS
Cleaver, meat mallet, small heavy frying pan, or Tigger (all optional)

In a small bowl, combine the whole-grain and Dijon mustards, vinegar, and sugar. Set aside.

Using a vegetable peeler or sharp knife, peel off and discard any tough, stringy parts of the outside and edges of the celery stalks. On a chopping board, working with one stalk at a time, put the flat side of a cleaver or large knife on the celery with the blade facing away from you, holding the handle with your non-dominant hand. Using your dominant hand, make a fist and smash the bottom of it onto the flat side of the knife, staying away from the sharp edge of the blade. (If that makes you nervous, use the flat side of a meat mallet, the bottom of a small heavy frying pan, or a rolling pin to smash the celery.) The celery should crack and flatten a bit. Repeat along the whole length of the celery. Cut the celery crosswise on a diagonal into 4-centimetre-long pieces and place into a medium bowl. Repeat with the remaining celery. Add the celery leaves and dressing to the bowl and toss, coating the celery evenly. Transfer to a serving bowl.

Tips for Success
- When choosing a head of celery, look for a firm one with lots of fresh, tender, light green leaves on the outer ribs and yellow leaves in the centre of the head.
- The salad will soften over time as it sits.

Green Couscous

When one must prepare for a long adventure (as Rabbit must have mustered himself when Christopher Robin needed saving from the Backson, or when he led a great effort to house poor Eeyore), even a salad can be fortified for more enduring energy (without losing its healthful or sensible qualities).

Though he would not have time to bother with learning nonsense about 'fibre', 'carb o'hydrates', or 'pro teens', Rabbit would nonetheless enjoy how the balance of those things in the small, fluffy pasta known as couscous could create a more densely nourishing salad to support those extended expeditions. This light but filling dish enhances the subtle flavours of couscous with vibrant lemon, a parade of aromatic herbs, nutty notes of toasted almonds, the peppery bite of rocket, and radishes.

YIELD: 4 servings

240 millilitres water
60 millilitres extra-virgin olive oil, divided
5 grams kosher (coarse) salt
170 grams couscous
2 large lemons
Freshly ground black pepper
4 spring onions, thinly sliced on the diagonal
60 grams baby rocket, chopped
16 grams fresh mint leaves, chopped
6 grams fresh coriander leaves, chopped
10 grams fresh flat-leaf parsley leaves, chopped
2 or 3 medium radishes, julienned
38 to 58 grams slivered almonds, toasted (see Ingredients and Methods, page 168)

SPECIAL TOOL
Mandoline slicer with a julienne blade (optional)

In a medium saucepan, bring the water, 30 millilitres of oil, and salt to the boil over a high heat. Stir in the couscous, cover, and remove the pan from the heat. Let the couscous steam, undisturbed, until the water has been absorbed and the couscous has plumped up, 5 to 10 minutes.

Meanwhile, zest and juice the lemons. In a small bowl, mix the lemon juice with the remaining 30 millilitres of oil and set aside.

Fluff the couscous by gently scraping it with a fork in layers, breaking up any clumps. Transfer the couscous to a large bowl. Gently massage the couscous with your fingers to separate the grains. Add the lemon zest and pepper to taste. Drizzle the lemon juice mixture over the couscous and toss to coat evenly. Add the spring onions, rocket, mint, fresh coriander, and parsley and mix well. Adjust the seasonings as needed. Transfer the couscous to a serving bowl and garnish with the radishes and almonds.

Customise Your Couscous

- Couscous, a North African staple, is a pasta of itty-bitty rolled balls made of semolina dough.
- This dish is very customisable. Baby spinach can be swapped for rocket, herbs can be bumped up or omitted, or bulk it up with diced cucumbers and fresh or slow-roasted cherry tomatoes (see Tomato and Herbed Ricotta Galette page 83).

Grilled Asparagus with Green Goddess Dressing

For all Rabbit's love of a good vegetable, even he could appreciate an occasional recipe whose star—whose cause of celebration—was other things that might be added, instead. In search of some fresh ideas, Rabbit called upon his very learned friend Owl. What began as a simple question quickly tumbled into a lot of dizzying words about nature, and celebration, and therefore something called a 'god-ess,' which all the more confusingly became a discussion of salad dressing and ingredients, and soon Owl distracting himself with the thought of anchovies, and his own need to find a bit of breakfast. (Or dinner. It is terribly hard to remember which is which with owls.)

As best he could remember (or parse), Rabbit went home and prepared (roughly) this creamy, tangy, and herbed dressing generously poured on the verdant, sharp tastes of asparagus.

YIELD: 4 servings

- 60 grams mayonnaise
- 60 grams soured cream
- 2.3 grams anchovy paste
- 15 millilitres red wine vinegar
- 6 grams minced fresh chives
- 8 grams chopped fresh flat-leaf parsley leaves
- Freshly ground black pepper
- 450 grams medium asparagus (about 1 bunch)
- 30 millilitres extra-virgin olive oil
- 1.65 grams kosher (coarse) salt

In a small bowl, stir together the mayonnaise, soured cream, anchovy paste, vinegar, chives, and parsley. Stir in pepper to taste.

Arrange an oven shelf to the top position. Preheat the grill to high.

Trim the woody ends of the asparagus. On a baking tray, toss the asparagus with the oil, salt, and pepper to taste. Arrange the asparagus in an even layer down the centre of the tray.

Grill until the asparagus is tender and charred in spots, shaking the tray once or twice during grilling, 2 to 3 minutes.

Serve the asparagus with the green goddess dressing.

Tips for Success
- Watch the asparagus carefully, as thicker or thinner stalks will cook at different rates.
- Any leftover sauce is delicious with other vegetables or even as a salad dressing.

Rabbit's Garden

Eeyore's Rainbow Veggie and Hummus Tray

Pooh had once heard the expression 'Sometimes there is no pleasing some people.' In pondering its meaning, he rather felt it would be truer to say 'Sometimes there is no pleasing some Eeyores.' For even though his grey friend was always pleasant company, he often seemed so terribly displeased himself. When attempting, with Rabbit, to bring Eeyore a surprise little something from Rabbit's garden, the pair endlessly imagined rejections, reservations, or remarks Eeyore might grumble in response to anything they thought to prepare. Self-defeated, Rabbit resigned to simply deliver a bit of everything (and some hummus for good measure). When they finally presented him with a platter much like this one, Eeyore was, actually, very pleased. In fact, he hardly seemed grey at all when saying how touched he was they went to all the trouble, and that the rainbow it made really brightened his day.

If you have your own picky eater, let them surprise you (and themselves, perhaps) by letting them pick through an assortment of crisp, fresh garden favourites to find new favourites to pair with creamy homemade hummus.

YIELD: 4 to 6 servings

One 425-gram can chickpeas
1 clove garlic, smashed
30 millilitres freshly squeezed lemon juice
15 grams tahini (see Ingredients and Methods, page 168)
15 to 30 millilitres extra-virgin olive oil
Kosher (coarse) salt
Sumac, for sprinkling (see Ingredients and Methods, page 168)
Chopped fresh or roasted red peppers, for garnish
Pine nuts, toasted, for garnish (see Ingredients and Methods, page 168)
Assorted rainbow-coloured vegetables, cut into pieces, for dipping

SPECIAL TOOL
Food processor

In a medium saucepan, bring the chickpeas and their liquid to a simmer over a medium-high heat. Reduce the heat to a simmer and cook until they are very soft, about 10 minutes. Let cool to room temperature in their liquid.

With a slotted spoon, transfer the chickpeas to a food processor (reserving the cooking liquid) along with the garlic, lemon juice, and tahini. Process until smooth. With a rubber spatula, scrape down the sides. Add about 45 millilitres of the cooking liquid and process until creamy, adding more as needed. Scrape down the sides again. With the machine running, slowly drizzle in the olive oil. Stir in 1.65 grams of salt, or enough until it tastes good to you.

Divide the hummus amongst three small serving bowls. Top one with a sprinkle of sumac, one with roasted red peppers, and the last with toasted pine nuts.

Arrange the vegetables in a rainbow shape on a serving platter or chopping board. Serve with the hummus trio.

Eyeore

'Thanks for noticin' me.'

Though he may seem dour, Eeyore is always happy to be pleasantly surprised. Because he assumes the worst will happen, and that he will be forgotten, any time his friends think to include him, it raises Eeyore's spirits (relatively speaking). So brighten his grey day with these recipes created with Eeyore in mind.

RECIPES:

Honey Lemonade with
Mint Ice Cubes . . . . page 38

Eeyore's Rainbow Veggie
and Hummus Tray . . . . page 80

Eeyore's 'Thistle' Soup . . . . . . page 109

Cauliflower Cheese with
Pretzel Crust . . . . page 113

Cheese and Onion Pie . . . . . . page 126

Fusilli Pasta with Pistachio
Pesto and Peas . . . . page 137

Crumpet Antipasti Pizza . . . . page 149

Eeyore's Tails . . . . page 161

Tomato and Herbed Ricotta Galette

Even dear Rabbit would admit he can sometimes, on occasion, become short-tempered. But the hours spent working in his garden give him long times to think. And so often, his thoughts drift to the kindness of his friends and the many qualities about them Rabbit is grateful for.

With Winnie the Pooh, in particular, one can always rely on a kind of sweet softness, no matter the heat of the moment or one's occasionally crusty exterior. Whether thoughts of Pooh Bear inspired or were the result of this dish, one can hardly recall. But the colourful similarity to the sweet yellow bear in the little red shirt is all the more fitting a tribute with its soft, herbed ricotta cheese heart. The roasted tomatoes achieve their own gentle sweetness inside the rustic, soft underbelly.

YIELD: One 25-centimetre galette (2 to 4 servings)

DOUGH
135 grams plain flour, plus more for dusting
4 grams sugar
1.65 grams kosher (coarse) salt
0.5 gram freshly ground black pepper
113 grams (1 stick) very cold unsalted butter, diced small
45 to 60 millilitres ice water

SLOW-ROASTED TOMATOES
One 285-gram container red grape or cherry tomatoes, halved lengthways
One 285-gram container yellow grape or cherry tomatoes, halved lengthways
8 thyme sprigs
2 cloves garlic, smashed
30 millilitres extra-virgin olive oil
1.65 grams kosher (coarse) salt
Freshly ground black pepper

RICOTTA FILLING
225 grams whole-milk ricotta cheese
2.5 grams finely chopped fresh basil
3 grams finely chopped fresh chives
10 millilitres extra-virgin olive oil
1 gram picked fresh thyme leaves
2 grams freshly grated lemon zest
0.8 gram kosher (coarse) salt
Freshly ground black pepper

ASSEMBLY
1 large egg, beaten with a splash of water
Thinly sliced fresh mint leaves

SPECIAL TOOLS
Food processor
Small offset spatula

To make the dough: In a food processor, combine the flour, sugar, salt, and pepper. Pulse a couple of times to mix. Scatter the butter over the flour mixture and pulse until it looks sandy. Add 45 millilitres of ice water and pulse until it looks like coarse wet sand and sticks together when pinched. Add more water if necessary. Pour the mixture onto a long sheet of clingfilm (about 35 centimetres long), gather it into a ball, and flatten it into a circle. Top with another long sheet of clingfilm and roll the dough into an 20-centimetre-diameter circle. You should see bits of butter strewn throughout the dough. Wrap the dough in the clingfilm and refrigerate it for at least 1 hour. Let it sit at room temperature for about 10 minutes before assembling.

To make the slow-roasted tomatoes: Preheat the oven to 135°C, or gas mark 1. Line a baking tray with baking paper. Arrange the red and yellow tomatoes cut sides up in a single layer on opposite sides of the prepared baking tray. Tuck the thyme and garlic into the tomatoes. Drizzle with the oil, then sprinkle with the salt and pepper to taste. Roast until the tomatoes are slightly wrinkled but still juicy, about 45 minutes. Set the tomatoes aside, discarding the thyme and garlic. Raise the oven temperature to 200°C, or gas mark 6.

Continued on page 85.

To make the ricotta filling: In a small bowl, combine the ricotta, basil, chives, oil, thyme, lemon zest, salt, and pepper to taste. Set aside.

To assemble and serve: Lightly dust a sheet of baking paper with flour. Place the dough on the baking—it will make it easier to transfer the crust to the baking tray. Roll out the dough into a 31.75-centimetre-diameter circle, about 3 millimetres thick. Slide the baking with the crust onto a baking tray. Don't worry if the edges peek over the sides of the tray.

Using a small offset spatula, spread the ricotta mixture onto the dough, allowing a 4-centimetre border from the edge. Arrange the red tomatoes cut sides up in a wide stripe in the middle of the galette. Fill in the space above and below the red stripe with the yellow tomatoes cut sides up. Fold the edges of the dough over the tomatoes. It should look rustic. Brush the crust with the egg wash.

Bake until the edges of the crust are golden brown and the bottom of the galette is nicely browned, 45 to 50 minutes. Remove the galette from the oven and let cool for 5 to 10 minutes. Sprinkle with mint leaves before serving.

Tips for Success

- Slow-roasting the tomatoes concentrates their flavour and brings out their sweetness.
- Cooking the tomatoes separately before assembling the galette removes moisture from the tomatoes, which can make the galette soggy.
- This galette is so light that two people can easily finish one. Maybe you should make two galettes—just to be safe.

Christopher Robin's Guide to Doing Nothing

When asked what he likes to do more than anything, Pooh, of course, chooses visiting Christopher Robin (particularly the bit where his friend offers him a smackerel of honey).

In Christopher Robin's opinion, though, the ideal activity is doing nothing. If you (like Pooh) are unsure of how, precisely, to do nothing, here is a friendly guide:

STEP 1: Someone (usually a grown-up) asks you what you are going to do for the day.

STEP 2: You tell them, 'Nothing.'

STEP 3: Then you go out and do it.

Tip

One can enjoy doing nothing alone, but like most things, doing nothing is often more enjoyable with friends.

Smoked Paprika Baked Acorn Squash

The list of things sweet little Piglet is afraid of includes (but is by no means limited to) the dark, thunder, lightning, very strong wind, woozles, Heffalumps, a great height, too deep a hole, and trying new foods. The last of those being first amongst reasons he usually eats haycorns. The small seedlings are a fine fit for his small appetite and are rarely surprising or unpredictable in any distressing sort of way.

It was only due to his mishearing this dish as baked 'haycorn' squash that Piglet fearlessly tasted a bite. (Though he did worry whatever squashed the haycorns might squash him next.)

Piglet was so delighted by the roasted, sweet, and nutty flavour (finished with rich butter and slight smoky spice of paprika), that he was hardly terrified to learn he had unwittingly tried something new.

YIELD: 4 servings

- 2 acorn squash
- 56 grams unsalted butter, melted
- 2.3 grams smoked paprika
- 1.65 grams kosher (coarse) salt, divided

Preheat the oven to 190°C, or gas mark 5.

Cut the squash in half through the stem end with a heavy, sharp knife. Scoop out the seeds and scrape out the strings (a grapefruit spoon works great for this job). Cut a small sliver from the skin side so the squash halves sit flat. With a sharp paring knife, carefully score the flesh. Arrange in a large shallow oven dish.

In a small bowl, stir together the butter and paprika. Brush all over the squash so the flesh doesn't dry out. If there is extra butter, divide it amongst the cavities. Sprinkle each with 1.65 grams of salt. Pour a little water into the oven dish (this prevents sticking or burning). Bake for about 30 minutes, then baste the surface with the paprika butter from the cavity. Continue baking until the squash is tender when poked with a fork and the edges are browned, another 15 to 30 minutes, depending on the size of the squash.

Veggie Chilli-Stuffed Jacket Potatoes

Few children (or grown-ups with childlike qualities, perhaps) share Rabbit's excitement upon hearing the word *vegetables*. Yet being the versatile and enriching things they are, vegetables can, in fact, be made into something to excite nearly anyone. For Roo, this particular preparation packs excitement into a relatable cosy pouch.

The festive assortment of peppers, tomato, onions, carrots, and beans is enriched by a playland of spices. One can challenge themselves by dialing up the heat (with optional jalapeños or other hot peppers) or splash into extra soured cream and cheese for cooling relief. All these dynamic tastes are at home inside a protective, warm potato jacket that make for a crisp and comforting finish.

YIELD: 4 servings

- 4 medium russet potatoes (about 1 kilogram)
- 30 millilitres neutral oil, plus more for baking
- 1 large carrot, chopped (about 150 grams)
- 1 medium onion, chopped (about 160 grams)
- 1 large red pepper, chopped (about 150 grams)
- 4 cloves garlic, chopped (about 20 grams)
- 2.3 grams ground cumin
- 2 grams ground coriander
- 2.3 grams paprika
- 0.5 gram dried oregano
- 3.3 grams kosher (coarse) salt
- Freshly ground black pepper
- One 440-gram can pinto beans, rinsed and drained
- One 410-gram can fire-roasted diced tomatoes
- 77.5 grams sweetcorn kernels, fresh or thawed if frozen
- 30 millilitres pickled jalapeño juice (optional)

TOPPINGS
- Shredded cheese (cheddar or jack)
- Soured cream
- Sliced spring onions
- Pickled jalapeño slices (optional)

Preheat the oven to 190°C, or gas mark 5.

Rub the potatoes with a little oil just to lightly coat the jackets and place them directly on the oven shelf. (No need to poke holes in them.) Put a baking tray below the potatoes to catch any drips. Bake until cooked all the way through, about 1 hour, depending on the size of the potatoes.

Meanwhile, pour the oil in a large saucepan or Dutch oven over medium-high heat. Add the carrot, onion, red pepper, and garlic and cook, stirring occasionally, until softened, 5 to 8 minutes, lowering the heat if the vegetables are sticking. Sprinkle in the cumin, coriander, paprika, oregano, salt, and pepper to taste and cook for 30 seconds. Add the beans, tomatoes with their juices, and sweetcorn and bring to a simmer. Then lower the heat to maintain a simmer, partially cover, and cook until the vegetables are softer and the tomato juices thicken, stirring occasionally, about 30 minutes. Stir in the pickled jalapeño juice (if using). Keep warm until needed.

When the potatoes are done, split them open in the middle lengthways. Lightly mash the potato flesh, sprinkle with salt as desired, and stir together. Fill each potato with about 200 grams of the veggie chilli. Top with cheese, soured cream, spring onions, and pickled jalapeño slices (if using).

Trio of Quick Pickles

On dreary days of heavy rain, many a hope is spoilt. Had Christopher Robin hoped to adventure in the Wood, he may not. As Rabbit had likely hoped to tend to his vegetables, he must wait. And though Winnie the Pooh undoubtedly hoped to visit a friend and eventually have them offer him something to eat . . . he won't. So, on those very days, do think of the vegetables, waiting for purpose, with no coming company to nourish. And for want of a Thing to Do, return to this page to preserve those kind, fresh radishes, courgettes, and onions by preparing them to become their deeply seasoned, brined, pickled versions as snacks and accentuations to feed your friends when you may gather again some sunnier day.

YIELD: Three 380-millilitre jars pickles

1 small bunch radishes
1 small courgette
1 small red onion
3 small dill sprigs
0.5 gram celery seeds
0.5 gram fennel seeds
2 dried whole red chillies
2 grams coriander seeds
1.1 grams ground turmeric
2 small bay leaves, fresh or dried
3.7 grams mustard seeds
1 gram caraway seeds
475 millilitres white vinegar
350 millilitres water
25 grams sugar
20 grams kosher (coarse) salt

SPECIAL TOOLS
Three 380-millilitre jars

Trim, then halve or quarter the radishes. Trim the courgette and cut into matchsticks about 9 centimetres long and 12 millimetres thick (your call if you want to pickle the matchsticks that just have the seeds—they taste fine but get softer than the others). Trim both ends of the onion and remove the peel. Slice the onion about 12 millimetres thick with the grain (from end to end).

Into one 380-millilitre jar (a peanut butter–size jar), put the dill, celery seeds, and fennel seeds. Into a second jar, put the dried chillies, coriander seeds, and turmeric. Into a third jar, put the bay leaves, mustard seeds, and caraway seeds. Put the radishes into the first jar, the courgette into the second, and the onion into the third.

In a large saucepan, bring the vinegar, water, sugar, and salt to the boil over a high heat, then whisk just to dissolve.

Pour a third of the brine over each vegetable. (The courgette matchsticks might bob in the liquid and not be totally covered. This is fine). Gently stir or swirl the brine so the flavourings get distributed. Let cool to room temperature and then seal and refrigerate overnight. The pickles will keep for about two months under refrigeration.

Rabbit's Smoothie

Of course, after hours under the garden sun, even Rabbit (or any rabbit) must occasionally divert from eating glorious fruits and vegetables to sustain oneself with a refreshing drink.

Fortunately, one may also drink those same fruits and vegetables.

This particular blend layers mild, vitamin-rich fresh spinach with the bright juiciness of blueberries and the deep, rich sweetness of dates. Such a cool and quick rush of nutrition will have you ready to garden again in no time.

YIELD: 4 servings

- 170 grams baby spinach (about 6 ounces)
- 120 millilitres cold water
- 12 pitted Deglet Noor dates
- 1.65 grams kosher (coarse) salt
- 930 grams frozen blueberries, divided

NOTE: *Using frozen blueberries is not only budget-friendly, but it also helps keep the smoothie cold. Add ice cubes to the smoothie if using fresh berries.*

SPECIAL TOOL
Blender

In a blender, combine the spinach and water and blend on the smoothie setting or high speed until mostly smooth. Add the dates and salt and blend until mostly smooth. Add 310 grams of blueberries and blend. Add another 310 grams of blueberries and blend. Add the final 310 grams of blueberries and blend until smooth. Adjust the thickness of the smoothie by adding water to loosen or ice cubes to thicken.

NOTE: *Blending in stages helps avoid the blender getting stopped up.*

Rabbit's Garden

Chapter 4

Holidays in the Hundred-Acre Wood

Within the Hundred-Acre Wood, holidays are celebrated much like they are anywhere else, except for the fact that they may happen any time at all.

Though they may follow the cues of a change of the season (and land their festivities in roughly the right time), Winnie the Pooh and his friends may just as likely decide to celebrate some nominal holiday on a Tuesday in May simply because the spirit so strikes them. (As is the wont of creatures unencumbered by calendars or Somewhere to Be on Monday.)

Shared, then, are a smattering of morsels to liven up your own special days, whether you choose merely to bring the inspiration of Pooh and friends on the appointed date or let them inspire you to bring a holiday celebration to any date you choose.

Guava and Soft Cream Cheese Hearts

The residents of the Hundred-Acre Wood hardly wait for a holiday to show their gratitude and affection for one another. But on Valentine's Day, the little signs of appreciation certainly take a more festive form. A particular favourite of Kanga and Roo is to enjoy a morning baking together (for the time with each other is its own loving celebration), then a hop around the Wood to deliver little treats such as these.

These heart-shaped guava and soft cream cheese puffs are unique and vibrant handmade treats that truly stand out. The natural tropical sweetness of guava melts into the rich soft cream cheese, filling the crisp and buttery pastry crust. A final dusting of sugar makes the gesture extra sweet, for friends and loved ones alike.

YIELD: About 15 pastries

- Plain flour, for dusting
- One 490.4-gram box frozen puff pastry, thawed (see Ingredients and Methods, page 168)
- Fifteen 6-millimetre-thick-by-2.5-centimetre-square slices guava paste (about 75 grams) (see Ingredients and Methods, page 168)
- Fifteen 6-millimetre-thick-by-2.5-centimetre-square slices soft cream cheese (about 60 grams)
- 1 large egg, beaten with a splash of water
- Demerara sugar, turbinado sugar, or sanding sugar, for sprinkling

SPECIAL TOOLS
- 7-centimetre heart-shaped biscuit cutter
- Pastry brush
- Small offset spatula

Line two baking trays with baking paper and set aside.

Place a sheet of baking paper on your work surface and lightly dust with flour. Unfold one sheet of puff pastry on the baking, keeping the other sheet in its wrapper in the fridge. Roll out the puff pastry into a 26.6-centimetre square. Cut the pastry into about 15 hearts, making sure to cut completely through. (Cut the hearts close together.) Transfer to a prepared baking tray in a single layer as done. Put in the fridge to chill. Repeat with the other sheet of puff pastry, transferring to the other prepared baking tray.

Preheat the oven to 200°C, or gas mark 6.

Stack a square of guava paste on top of each square of soft cream cheese. Lightly brush the edge of a heart with the egg wash. Use a small offset spatula to put a guava-and-cheese stack in the middle of the heart. Top with an unbrushed heart and gently press the edges together. Press the tines of a fork around the edges to seal the pastry. Transfer the assembled heart to one of the baking trays. Repeat with the remaining pastry, guava stacks, and egg wash. Put the baking tray in the freezer and chill until the pastries are firm, about 15 minutes.

Brush the egg wash over the tops of the chilled hearts and sprinkle with sugar. Use the tip of a paring knife to cut two slits in the top of each pastry to allow steam to escape. Bake, rotating halfway through, until the pastry is deep golden brown, about 25 minutes. The filling, fresh out of the oven, will be very hot and can cause burns. Let the pastries cool for at least 15 minutes before serving.

> **Pastry Inspiration**
>
> These pastries, called *pastelitos de guayaba y queso*, are popular in Cuban and other Latin bakeries.

Chocolate Bark with Pretzels and Dried Cranberries

Valentine sweets need not always evoke the heart to show love and appreciation. When Christopher Robin first saw a 'chocolate bark' much like this one, it reminded him of a lovely afternoon playing 'Poohsticks,' a game his silly old bear had invented (accidentally, as many things happen with Pooh). It seemed funny how a chocolate can remind him of a stick, which can remind him of a happy memory with friends. But he was glad of it.

You can make your own Chocolate Bark to enjoy the salty-sweet mix of crunchy pretzels and rich dark chocolate, adorned with tart and chewy dried cranberries. Perhaps a perfect snack to bring on a trip to play Poohsticks with a loved one and make a new fond memory of your own.

YIELD: 4 servings

- One 285-gram bag dark chocolate morsels
- 15 millilitres neutral oil
- About 30 grams dried cranberries
- About 20 grams thin pretzel sticks, broken into pieces

SPECIAL TOOLS
Large offset spatula

Line a baking tray with baking paper.

In a medium microwave-safe bowl, melt the chocolate morsels and oil in the microwave in 30-second intervals, stirring after each interval, until just barely melted. It should only take two or three times.

Tip the chocolate onto the prepared baking tray, scraping the bowl with a rubber spatula. Using a large offset spatula, spread the chocolate on the paper into a thin, even layer. Sprinkle with cranberries and pretzel pieces, pressing firmly to adhere. Refrigerate until firm.

Break into big pieces. Store in an airtight container.

How to Play Poohsticks

At a stream, creek, or other such moving water, players find a stick of their choosing. When on top of a bridge (or at the side of the water) players drop their sticks into the stream at the same time, then rush to see which stick appears out the other end of the bridge (or reaches a pre-appointed point downstream) first.

Beetroot-Dyed Deviled Eggs

Should you plan to spend Easter with your friends from the Hundred-Acre Wood, keep in mind Tigger's most competitive spirit. If one is hiding eggs for smaller guests to discover, one may want to account for the likelihood that Tigger will not be able to resist finding the most eggs faster than any other. Perhaps if one announces the game when the only eggs in sight are these, Tigger may soon withdraw himself from the competition.

These festively coloured eggs are packed with unexpected spicy-and-soured flavours. (Though tiggers prefer the sweetness of malted syrup or, likely, the holiday's malted eggs.) Soaked in a pickled-beetroot vinegar, the now-pink egg whites have a beautiful hue. The deviled-egg filling blends egg yolk with soothing soured cream and mayo and the spicy tang of hot English mustard.

One swiftly seized egg should be all it takes to soured (and spice) Tigger's appetite for victory, leaving the hidden malted eggs for your Roos and Piglets and the rest of these dynamically tasty snacks for the more developed palates in your party.

YIELD: 12 deviled eggs

6 large eggs
One 450-gram jar mini pickled beetroots
180 millilitres apple cider vinegar
120 millilitres water
20 grams kosher (coarse) salt
12.5 grams sugar
1.5 grams cumin seeds
1.5 grams black peppercorns
5 allspice berries
45 grams mayonnaise
45 grams soured cream
5 to 10 grams dried English mustard

NOTE: *English mustard packs a sinus-clearing punch, which is why we've suggested a range. Start at the lower end to see how you like it and add more from there if you can take the heat.*

Put the eggs in a medium saucepan and cover with water. Bring to the boil over a high heat. Once the water just comes to the boil, cover the pan and remove from the heat. Set a timer for 10 minutes. Once the timer goes off, drain the eggs and rinse under cold water (or put into an ice bath). Once cooled, peel the eggs and put into a medium bowl.

Pour the pickled beetroot juice into the same saucepan. (Reserve all but one of the beetroots for another use.) Add the vinegar, water, salt, sugar, cumin seeds, peppercorns, and allspice to the pan. Bring the liquid to the boil over a medium-high heat just to dissolve the sugar, 1 to 2 minutes. Pour the brine over the eggs and let cool. Then refrigerate for 6 to 24 hours, depending on how colourful you want the eggs to be.

Halve the eggs and carefully pop out the yolks into a medium bowl. Arrange the whites on a platter. With a fork, mash the yolks with the mayonnaise, soured cream, and mustard. Spoon or pipe the filling evenly into the whites. Top each with a slice of beetroot.

Holidays in the Hundred-Acre Wood

Tigger

'T-T-F-N: ta-ta for now!'

Full of boundless energy, bounce, and confidence—tiggers truly are wonderful things. (As Tigger himself will tell you.) Yet they can be very picky eaters, so be sure to prepare one of these Tigger-approved recipes if you hope to keep him at the table long enough for a proper meal.

RECIPES:

Honey Apple Cupcakes with Honey Soft Cream Cheese Frosting . . . . page 33

Smashed Celery Salad with Grainy Mustard Dressing . . . . page 75

Chilli Cornbread Casserole . . page 139

Tigger-Striped Biscuits . . . . . page 154

Malted Ice-Cream Sundae with Mini Malted Mochi . . . . page 162

Basque Cheesecake with Orange Blossom Honey

Dark, deceiving appearances that, in the end, reveal kindly-given sweet surprises—such a turn is what makes Halloween both exciting and delighting. (Though poor Piglet still prefers to stay inside until the spooky things are over with.) For those uninterested in sweets, this dessert fits the occasion.

Beneath the blackened-mirror or 'cursed pie' appearance lies the joyous reveal of a creamy cheesecake whose bites unmask rich tones of honey (for Pooh) and fragrant orange.

YIELD: One 23-centimetre cake

- 4 large eggs
- Three 225-gram packages soft cream cheese, cut into chunks
- 12 grams freshly grated orange zest
- 150 grams sugar
- 160 grams orange blossom honey
- 10 millilitres vanilla essence
- 1.65 grams kosher (coarse) salt
- 180 millilitres double cream
- 32 grams cornflour

SPECIAL TOOLS

- Food processor (2.6-litre minimum)
- 23-centimetre springform pan
- Digital instant-read thermometer (optional)
- Cake plate

Preheat the oven to 245°C, or gas mark 9. Fit a baking tray with a wire rack. Use your hands to crumple up a long (about 40-centimetre) sheet of baking paper into a tight ball. Unwad the paper, flatten it out, and line a 23-centimetre springform tin with it, pressing it into the corners of the pan. Let the excess hang over the sides of the tin. Repeat with an additional one or two sheets of baking paper, crisscrossing over the first sheet, to fully cover the bottom and sides of the tin. Place the tin on the prepared baking tray.

In a large food processor, blend the eggs, soft cream cheese, orange zest, sugar, honey, vanilla, and salt for 30 seconds. Add the double cream and continue to process, scraping down the sides once or twice, until the batter is silky smooth, 2 to 3 minutes. (If your soft cream cheese is cold, you may need to blend longer to remove all the lumps.) Sift the cornflour into the bowl and process until combined. Pour into the prepared tin.

Bake the cake, rotating halfway through, until the top is a burnished brown and the cake is still jiggly (but not sloshy), 30 to 35 minutes. (You can also check by inserting a digital thermometer into the cake—it's ready when it reads 85°C.) Let the cake cool completely on a wire shelf.

Release the sides of the tin, then transfer the cake, including the baking paper if you'd like, to a cake plate. Carefully peel the paper away from the cake and serve.

Continued on page 105.

Tips for Success

- If chilling the cake, pop it into the fridge, uncovered, for 8 hours or overnight. Bring it to room temperature before serving.
- Orange blossom honey is light and floral with a citrusy flavour and aroma, but any mild blossom honey can be used. In this cheesecake, the flavour of orange blossom honey is strongest when the cake is served at room temperature, prior to any chilling.

Fun Facts

- Basque cheesecake, aka burnt Basque cheesecake, from the Basque region of Spain is lighter and creamier than New York–style cheesecake. This rustic-looking cake puffs up like a soufflé during baking but collapses as it cools. The dark top gives it a caramelised flavour.
- Basque cheesecake is unfussy—no crust, water bath, or overnight chill necessary, and in our recipe, the cheese, eggs, and cream don't need to be brought to room temperature before baking.

Not-Too-Spooky Halloween Fun

If you wish to throw a Halloween celebration for little ones like Roo or skittish friends like Piglet, here are some of their favourite scare-less festive activities.

Pumpkin Painting: All the fun of carving a jack-o'-lantern, without the nervousness of using sharp carving tools.

Daylight Reverse Trick-or-Treating: Make a trip to visit friends, family, or local shops to show off your costumes. Bring sweets for them and let it be a pleasant surprise if they have a treat for you.

Tales of Friendly Monsters: Enjoy a nice story about a misunderstood 'monster' or create your own (about a friendly woozle, perhaps?).

Witches' Brew

Whereas young Roo is excited for scares on a Halloween night, Kanga knows such a little heart can handle only so much fright. Small shivers are best balanced against bigger fun. For a creepy surprise in your celebration (that quickly turns to giggles, of course), dip into a cauldron of this Witches' Brew.

Guests drawn to this potion of sweet, fizzy punch will be startled to find wriggly worms bobbing on the surface! But on realising they are just the gummy variety, all will enjoy the cran-raspberry tart-sweetness and ginger ale bubbling its way through. Melting raspberry sorbet in the mix supports the fruity rush to the taste buds and adds swirls of colours for the eye, both to magical effect.

YIELD: 8 to 10 servings

About 10 gummy worms, plus more for serving
One 1.9-litre bottle cran-raspberry juice, chilled
475 millilitres ginger ale, chilled
475 millilitres raspberry sorbet

SPECIAL TOOLS
25-centimetre fluted Bundt pan
3.8-litre punch bowl
7-gram biscuit scoop

Arrange the gummy worms in the bottom of a Bundt pan and fill with water just to cover the worms. Freeze until solid.

In a 3.8-litre punch bowl, pour in the cran-raspberry juice. Run the bottom of the Bundt pan under warm water to loosen the ice ring from the pan. Float the ice ring with the worms facing up in the juice. Using a 7-gram biscuit scoop, scoop balls of the sorbet into the juice. Pour the ginger ale into the bowl. Ladle the punch into cups. Drape a (non-frozen) gummy worm over the rim, if desired.

Eeyore's 'Thistle' Soup

In planning an autumn-time gathering of gratitude (a 'Giving of Thanks,' in other words), the friends who reside in the Hundred-Acre Wood paused to consider Eeyore.

Realising he had no place to prepare food himself (a house made of leaned sticks had neither a pantry nor kitchen), a dish he would enjoy must come from them. Ideally (for Eeyore), something with thistles—as it was the donkey's usual choice—but ideally for everyone else, something not so pointy and troubling to eat as thistles are.

Eeyore's 'Thistle' Soup was born that day out of their sense of togetherness, joining the largest pointy plant they found in Rabbit's garden (in truth, an artichoke, though the details hardly matter) with a stock of ingredients to make it a less prickly dish they could all be thankful for, together.

The result is a lightly nutty, earthy, and buttery bowl that warms the body just as sharing it warms the spirit.

YIELD: 4 to 6 servings (about 1.4 litres)

- 56 grams unsalted butter, divided
- 1 medium onion, chopped (about 160 grams)
- 3 cloves garlic, minced
- Kosher (coarse) salt
- Three 400-gram cans artichoke quarters, drained
- 700 millilitres low-sodium chicken stock or vegetable stock, plus more as needed
- 120 millilitres double cream
- 12 to 18 grams chopped fresh chives (2.5-centimetre pieces)
- 2 slices sandwich bread, cut into 2-centimetre cubes

SPECIAL TOOL
Blender

In a Dutch oven, melt 28 grams of butter over medium-high heat. Add the onion, garlic, and a pinch of salt and cook until soft but not browned, about 5 minutes. Add the artichokes and stock, cover, and bring to a simmer (the stock should just cover the artichokes). Cook until the artichokes are very soft, about 10 minutes.

Transfer the soup to a blender, in batches if necessary. With the lid slightly ajar and covered with a clean tea towel, purée the soup until smooth. Rinse the Dutch oven and return the soup to the pot. Stir in the cream and 1.65 grams of salt. Adjust the consistency with more stock as needed. Keep the soup on low heat while you make the croutons.

In a medium frying pan, melt the remaining 28 grams of butter over a medium-high heat. Add the bread cubes and toast, stirring and tossing, until golden, adjusting the heat to prevent them burning, about 8 minutes.

Ladle the soup into bowls and garnish with the chives and buttery croutons.

NOTE: *Garnish with chive blossoms when in season (late spring/early summer).*

Stilton Toasts with Roasted Grapes

In the gifting holidays, a Piglet of modest means can nonetheless forage a dish to give his friends. These appetisers take harvested grapes (for Rabbit) and puncture their sweet flavour by roasting them with fresh sprigs of thyme (for brush-eating Eeyore). The creamy and salty Stilton cheese provides sophisticated flavour for discerning Kanga, on bite-size servings perfect for little Roo. Topping it all off with stripes of flavoured honey makes it a thoughtful acknowledgement of Tigger and Pooh, too.

YIELD: 4 servings

- 680 grams red seedless grapes on the vine
- 15 millilitres extra-virgin olive oil, plus more for brushing
- 0.4 gram kosher (coarse) salt
- Freshly ground black pepper
- 8 small thyme sprigs
- ½ baguette (about 30 centimetres long)
- 225 grams Stilton cheese, at room temperature

Preheat the oven to 220°C, or gas mark 7. Line a baking tray with foil.

On the prepared baking tray, toss the grapes with the oil, salt, and pepper to taste. Nestle the thyme sprigs in the grapes. Roast until the grapes begin to burst and char, 20 to 25 minutes. Discard the thyme sprigs.

While the grapes are roasting, slice the baguette into 12-millimetre slices on the diagonal. Arrange on a second baking tray. Brush with olive oil. Once the grapes come out of the oven, slide the baking tray with the bread slices into the oven and toast until the bread is lightly browned, about 5 minutes.

Pile the toasts into a basket. Arrange the grapes on a chopping board with the Stilton. To serve, spread a little of the cheese onto a toast and top with a few grapes.

> **Tips for Success**
> - Drizzle the toasts with a little hot honey or rosemary honey (see page 21).
> - The grapes are best eaten warm, and they pop off the vine a little easier as well.
> - The grapes may leave a stain on a wooden chopping board, so either place them on a small sheet of baking paper or use a non-porous surface.

Cauliflower Cheese with Pretzel Crust

Blistery, blustery winter holidays call for a hearty and heating dish that can warm your guests straight in from the cold.

Whereas Rabbit had intended this creamy and revivingly seasoned cauliflower casserole to be held until the proper mealtime, an arriving Eeyore grumbled so thoroughly about the effects of trudging through snow that his harried host surrendered and offered up a piping-hot dish to warm his nose and busy his mouth.

Eeyore savored (and nearly smiled at) the rich buttery taste of melted cheeses and creams and flavourful heat from English mustard, a peppercorn and clove-infused cream sauce, and the savoury tang of Worcestershire. The welcoming serving lifted Eeyore's spirits so quickly that, on subsequent occasions, Rabbit made sure to have a batch ready for his grey friend—with pretzels atop like a little stick cabin, to make Eeyore feel at home.

YIELD: 4 to 6 main or 8 side dish servings

Kosher (coarse) salt
½ small onion, cut into 2 wedges
1 bay leaf, fresh or dried
3 whole black peppercorns
1 whole clove
950 millilitres milk
1 large cauliflower (about 1.1 kilograms)
115 grams extra sharp cheddar cheese, preferably an aged English farmstead variety, if available
60 grams Parmesan cheese
56 grams unsalted butter, cut into pats, plus 14 grams, melted
45 grams plain flour
6 grams dry English mustard
10 millilitres Worcestershire sauce
60 grams roughly crushed thin pretzel sticks

SPECIAL TOOLS
Cheesecloth
Kitchen string

Preheat the oven to 220°C, or gas mark 7. Bring a large saucepot of well-salted water to the boil over a high heat. (Don't be shy with the salt, because the cauliflower is rather bland and needs the boost.)

Enclose the onion wedges, bay leaf, peppercorns, and clove in a piece of cheesecloth and tie with kitchen string. In a medium saucepan, bring the milk and cheesecloth sachet just to a simmer over a medium heat, about 8 minutes, watching carefully towards the end so it doesn't boil over. Remove from the heat and let sit to infuse the milk while you prepare the cauliflower and cheeses.

Trim the cauliflower end and leaves and break or cut into large florets, including the stem if desired. Add the cauliflower to the boiling water, let it return to the boil, and cook until just tender, about another 2 minutes. Drain well, shaking off as much water as possible. Scatter the florets onto a large clean tea towel to absorb additional moisture. Wipe out the saucepot.

On the large holes of a box grater, shred the cheddar. Shred the Parmesan on the small holes. Reserve about 60 grams of each for topping.

Continued on page 114.

If the milk has cooled too much, give it a shot of heat so it begins to steam. In the same saucepan used to cook the cauliflower, melt the butter pats over a medium-low heat. Whisk in the flour a little at a time and cook, whisking occasionally, until it becomes a light tan paste and there's no longer a raw flour smell, 3 to 4 minutes. Remove the cheesecloth sachet from the milk, pressing to get out all the liquid. Slowly whisk the milk into the paste (also called a roux, but not our Roo) until it's smooth, and cook while continuing to whisk until the sauce begins to thicken, about 4 minutes. Remove from the heat and stir in the mustard and Worcestershire sauce. Add the cheese in handfuls and whisk into a smooth sauce. Season with 2.5 grams salt.

Add the cauliflower to the cheese sauce and gently stir to coat. Pour into a 23-by-33-centimetre oven (or at least a 2.8-litre dish or Dutch oven if using a high-sided dish). Scatter the reserved Parmesan and then cheddar cheese over top. Wipe the edges clean of any sauce to prevent it burning.

In a medium bowl, toss the pretzels with the melted butter and then scatter over the cauliflower. Bake until the sauce is bubbling and the cheese is golden in spots, about 20 minutes. Let stand for a few minutes before serving, as it's very hot.

Pizzelle Snowflakes

One cold winter's day that seemed it might be a holiday (though Winnie the Pooh wasn't sure which, so Tigger suggested it might be Tigger's Day), Roo assured them all very assuredly that it can't be a winter holiday when it wasn't snowing. So they all set about to make snow.

After many creative but unsuccessful efforts Rabbit proposed the only sensible consideration they had not yet considered . . . was to ask Owl. In his hollow-tree home, the wise old bird flittered through his many books until he gave them this. The definitive, scientific process for creating snow as OK'd by a co (short for company) from something called a 'Co OK Book.'

Though the results were not what Pooh (or Tigger, or Roo, or Rabbit) had expected, they were delicious. And the crisp, seasonally spiced, lightly sweet treats made the day feel quite like a holiday indeed.

YIELD: 2 to 4 dozen 13-centimetre pizzelle (depending on the griddle design)

- 3 large eggs
- 150 grams caster sugar
- 6 grams freshly grated orange zest
- 169 grams (1½ sticks) unsalted butter, melted and cooled
- 15 millilitres anise essence
- 5 millilitres vanilla essence
- 3.5 grams aniseed, toasted (optional, see Ingredients and Methods, page 168) and crushed
- 210 grams plain flour
- 9.2 grams baking powder
- 2.5 grams kosher (coarse) salt
- Neutral oil, for brushing
- Icing sugar, for dusting

SPECIAL TOOLS
- Electric non-stick 13-centimetre pizzelle maker
- Electric whisk
- Small offset spatula

In a large bowl, use an electric whisk to beat the eggs, caster sugar, and orange zest until thick, about 5 minutes. Add the butter, anise and vanilla essences, and aniseed and beat until combined. In a small bowl, whisk the flour, baking powder, and salt. Add the flour mixture to the egg mixture, 60 grams at a time, until the batter is completely smooth and thick like brownie batter.

Preheat the pizzelle maker until hot. Fit two baking trays with wire racks.

Depending on the design of the griddles, drop 15 to 30 grams of batter slightly above the centre of each griddle. If the design doesn't look like a snowflake, use about 15 grams of the batter so that the batter doesn't reach the edges and will look lacy. Close the machine and squeeze the handles together tightly. Secure the latch on the handle if your machine comes with one. Cook until the pizzelle are lightly browned, 45 to 60 seconds. (The cooking time will vary depending on the brand and model. Like pancakes, expect

Continued on page 117.

the first batch to be duds. If the pizzelle stick, lightly brush the griddles with a little neutral oil.) Using an offset spatula, gently transfer the pizzelle to the shelf as done. The pizzelle will be floppy but will firm up as they cool. Let the pizzelle maker reheat between batches. Repeat with the remaining batter. The biscuits can be stacked once they have completely cooled. Dust the pizzelle with icing sugar before serving so they look like snowflakes.

Tips for Success

- Pizzelle are light, crisp Italian waffle biscuits traditionally flavoured with anise. If you're not a fan of sweet licorice, feel free to use vanilla, lemon, and/or almond essences.
- Avoid making pizzelle in humid weather or the biscuits will get soft.

Roasted Vegetable Platter with Honey Butter Glaze

The best holidays offer occasions to show thought towards those we care about, over ourselves. In that spirit, one Christmas (or a like-minded day they had decided to celebrate with gift-giving) Pooh prepared to gift Rabbit some wild vegetables he had gathered. And Rabbit pulled down a jar of honey for Pooh. But Pooh feared vegetables seem rather unexciting on their own . . . and Rabbit questioned whether more honey alone was truly what Pooh needed . . . So when it came time to exchange gifts, each had prepared for the other some honey-covered vegetables.

Now they have asked to share that gift with you (with a few culinary refinements) in this golden-glazed and buttery preparation for sweet carrots and their earthier, nuttier-toned cousin parsnips. (Salted, peppered, and lightly herbed to your taste.)

YIELD: 4 to 6 servings

- 42 grams unsalted butter
- 40 grams honey
- 1 bunch slender carrots (about 340 grams), peeled if desired
- 4 parsnips (about 450 grams), as slender as you can find, peeled, trimmed, and halved lengthways
- 1.65 grams kosher (coarse) salt
- Freshly ground black pepper
- Chopped fresh coriander or flat-leaf parsley leaves, for garnish

Preheat the oven to 220°C, or gas mark 7.

In a small saucepan, melt the butter and honey over a medium heat. On a baking tray, toss the carrots and parsnips with the honey butter (the butter will congeal a little from the cooler vegetables, but that's ok). Sprinkle with the salt and pepper to taste and toss again to evenly coat. Spread out evenly on the tray. Roast until the vegetables are tender and the parsnips are golden, about 25 minutes.

Tips for Carrot Lovers

- If your carrots are slender and fresh, you may not need to peel the skin, as it's quite thin and full of nutrients.
- If you find carrots with their tops on, leave a few centimetres or so for a prettier presentation.
- Carrot tops can be made into pesto or chimichurri.

Holidays in the Hundred-Acre Wood

Lemon Posset Glazed with Marmalade

Christopher Robin knew it was truly the winter holidays when suddenly so many sweets and desserts abound that he could easily take extras to share with his friends in the Hundred-Acre Wood, and no grown-up would notice.

It was under these circumstances that Winnie the Pooh came to try something called Lemon Posset with Marmalade. Whereas Christopher Robin could not quite answer what it was, Pooh very much enjoyed its creamy, sweet, and dazzling citrusy taste—and for Christopher Robin to have shared it with him.

YIELD: 6 servings

700 millilitres double cream
250 grams sugar
12 grams freshly grated lemon zest
6 grams freshly grated orange zest
0.8 gram kosher (coarse) salt
75 millilitres freshly squeezed lemon juice
15 millilitres warm water, plus more as needed
60 to 80 grams marmalade

SPECIAL TOOLS
6 small glasses or ramekins (at least 180 millilitres each)

In a medium saucepan over a medium heat, combine the cream, sugar, lemon and orange zests, and salt and bring to a simmer. Do not allow the mixture to boil. Cook, stirring occasionally, until the sugar dissolves, about 10 minutes. Make sure the sugar is completely dissolved, or your posset will be grainy. Remove the pan from the heat. Whisk the lemon juice into the mixture then let cool for 10 minutes.

Give the mixture a gentle whisk to break up any clumps that may have formed and divide the mixture into six small glasses or ramekins. Cover each with clingfilm and chill in the refrigerator until set, about 3 hours.

Just before serving, in a small bowl, stir the warm water into the marmalade, then add a little more at a time to loosen it into a thin glaze. (It's up to you how much zest from the marmalade you want to include.) Spoon the mixture over the possets and spread to glaze. Serve.

What Is a Posset?

Posset is a creamy classic British dessert. Rather than using gelatin or egg yolks to thicken simmered cream, lemon juice is added to set it into a lush, smooth, bright, and citrusy custard.

Chapter 5
Suppers

Of all the meals each day offers (somehow Winnie the Pooh being offered more than most), suppers may encourage the most thought.

Breakfast, after all, is decided upon when one is barely awake enough to consider. Lunches are so often decided in a rush between the day's events as to simply be a matter of what is on hand. (And, for Pooh at least, all other rumbly tumblies are, of course, silenced with honey.)

So it is suppertime that calls for consideration. Does the day want for a little more adventure? Or did worrisome troubles or terrible tumbles leave you needing a warm comfort instead? Shall we gather with friends? (And what would they enjoy?) Or does tonight offer time to ourselves to reflect on all we have to be grateful for?

Whichever way the day finds you, your friends in the Hundred-Acre Wood share these next thoughts for food as food for thought.

Mushrooms on Toast

One versatile dish in any English household (the type from which Christopher Robin sets out) is that of Mushrooms on Toast. It can be made a centrepiece of a meal, to support a fine roast, or as a light repast all its own. Being a boy possessed of both great curiosity and a growing appetite, Christopher Robin learned to spot the right sorts of mushrooms to make a delicious toast, as they appear around the Hundred-Acre Wood. After favourable weather, he could return home (or to Kanga's) with pockets overflowing with enough mushrooms to make a feast of toasts for all.

Cooked mushrooms balance earthy and meaty flavours, here given a buttery texture and finish to top and soak into the base of your favourite bread. Cooked shallots add a caramelised sweetness, whereas sprinkled parsley adds a note of fresh herbs.

YIELD: 4 servings

- 84 grams unsalted butter, divided
- 680 grams mixed mushrooms (cremini, white button, shiitakes), cleaned (see Ingredients and Methods, page 168), sliced 6 millimetres thick, divided
- 1 large shallot, finely diced (about 60 grams)
- 5 grams kosher (coarse) salt
- Freshly ground black pepper
- 60 millilitres double cream
- 15 millilitres freshly squeezed lemon juice
- 12 grams chopped fresh flat-leaf parsley leaves
- 4 slices toast, buttered if you prefer

Heat two large frying pans over medium-high heat and melt 42 grams of butter in each pan. Add half of the mushrooms to each pan and toss to coat with the butter. Spread the mushrooms in an even layer, pushing some up the sides of the tins. Cook, undisturbed, until golden brown on the bottoms, about 5 minutes. Give them a stir and then let them cook undisturbed again. The mushrooms will release their liquid, which will then evaporate. Once evaporated, stir the mushrooms and cook until nicely browned all over, about another 3 minutes.

Transfer all the mushrooms to one pan and add the shallot, salt, and pepper to taste. Toss and cook another minute, stirring occasionally so the shallot doesn't burn. Stir in the cream and lemon juice to coat. They should be absorbed quickly. Stir in the parsley and adjust the seasonings as needed. Divide the toast amongst four plates, spoon mushrooms on each slice, and serve.

Suppers 125

Cheese and Onion Pie

If planning a dinner with Eeyore, he will, of course, insist you not go to too much trouble on his account. Perhaps a homemade classic Cheese and Onion Pie will be just what the donkey ordered? Especially if you use a ready-to-cook piecrust, the simple ingredients make for a more leisurely cooking experience than many a recipe. And when finished, the glistening golden crust is an understated but wholesome sight, which would look right at home outside Eeyore's home built from sticks. Nonetheless, the first bite shows that, just like Eeyore, the simple exterior is filled with warmth and love. In this case, a buttery, delicious favourite where the sautéed onions offer a rich sweet and savoury to weave throughout the creamy melted cheese.

YIELD: 4 to 6 servings

- 28 grams unsalted butter
- 1.6 kilograms yellow onions, very thinly sliced (4 or 5 very large onions)
- 3.3 grams kosher (coarse) salt
- Freshly ground black pepper
- One 399.7-gram box store-bought refrigerated piecrusts, at room temperature (see Ingredients and Methods, page 168)
- 225 grams extra-sharp cheddar cheese, grated
- 1 large egg, beaten with a splash of water

SPECIAL TOOLS
- 30-centimetre high-sided frying pan
- 23-centimetre deep-dish pie pan

Preheat the oven to 180°C, or gas mark 4.

In a 30-centimetre high-sided frying pan, melt the butter over a medium heat. Add the onions (it will seem like a lot and fill to the top, but they cook down considerably) and cover. Let steam, shaking the pan occasionally, until they soften somewhat so you can more easily stir them, 5 to 10 minutes. Stir in the salt and pepper to taste and continue cooking, covered, stirring occasionally, until the onions are very soft, about 30 minutes, turning the heat down if they start to brown or stick to the pan. Keeping the pan uncovered now, cook until the onions start to lightly stick to the pan, 5 to 10 minutes. Stir to unstick, then continue cooking, stirring occasionally, until most of the liquid evaporates and what's left clings to the onions, 10 to 15 more minutes. Spread out on a large plate or baking tray to cool.

Unfold one of the piecrusts and lay it in a 23-centimetre deep-dish pie pan. Spread one-third of the cheese on the crust, then half of the onions, another one-third of the cheese, the remaining onions, and top with the remaining cheese. Lay the second piecrust over top and gently press the dough around the edge of the filling to enclose. Then fold and decoratively crimp the edges to seal. Brush all over with the egg wash. Cut a few vents in the middle to allow steam to escape. Bake until the crust is golden brown, about 45 minutes. Cool for 10 minutes before serving. (This pie can be enjoyed warm or fully cooled.)

Asparagus, Potato, and Pecorino Frittata

When one works as tirelessly and attentively in their garden as Rabbit, success can mean a great many more vegetables than one rabbit can eat. In those seasons of abundance, to keep the fruits (and vegetables) of his labours from going to waste, Rabbit just as tirelessly delivers his harvests and encourages friends to eat like him for breakfast, lunch, and dinner!

If only Rabbit knew a fine frittata is a perfect way to pack auxiliary vegetables into a winning meal great for evenings, mornings, or anytime between. Here, verdant asparagus and soft potato pieces soak in the rich flavours of egg and tangy pecorino cheese. Savoury and satisfying in every slice, the frittata's flavours are easily enhanced with your favourite seasonings or hot sauces.

YIELD: 4 to 6 servings

- 2 medium Yukon Gold potatoes or other yellow potatoes
- 10 medium asparagus spears (about ¾ bunch)
- 8 large eggs
- 3.3 grams kosher (coarse) salt, divided
- Freshly ground black pepper
- 37.5 grams grated pecorino cheese
- 28 grams unsalted butter
- Hot sauce, for serving (optional)

SPECIAL TOOL
Thin flexible spatula (like a fish spatula)

Arrange an oven shelf to the second position from the top (about 15 centimetres away from the grill element). Preheat the grill to high.

Peel the potatoes. Cut them in half lengthways and then cut into about 6-millimetre slices. Arrange the slices on a large plate, but do not overlap. Cover the plate with clingfilm and microwave in 30-second increments for about 1½ minutes. If the potatoes are still not cooked through, microwave in 10-second increments until soft. Repeat with any remaining potatoes. (Cooking in short blasts keeps the potatoes from clumping together.)

Snap the woody ends from the asparagus. Slice the spears on the diagonal into 6- to 12-millimetre pieces.

In a medium bowl, whisk the eggs, 1.65 grams of salt, pepper to taste, and 30 grams of pecorino.

Melt the butter in a 30-centimetre ovenproof, grill-safe non-stick frying pan over medium-high heat, about 2 minutes. Once nearly melted, add the asparagus, 0.8 gram of salt, and pepper to taste. Cook, stirring occasionally, until crisp-tender, 4 to 5 minutes. Add the potatoes and

Continued on page 130.

Suppers 129

remaining 0.8 gram of salt and stir to coat. Pour in the eggs. With a rubber spatula, distribute the potato slices as evenly as possible. Push the eggs from the side and underneath while tilting and turning the frying pan to allow more eggs to flow underneath until they are almost set, lowering the heat if the eggs are browning too fast (but if they stick a little bit it's OK), about 3 minutes.

Sprinkle the remaining 7.5 grams of pecorino over the eggs. Put the frying pan under the grill until the eggs puff and turn light brown, about 2 minutes. (Carefully rotate the frying pan as needed to get the surface evenly browned.)

Use a thin flexible spatula to loosen the sides and bottom of the frittata from the frying pan. Cut into four to six wedges. Serve with hot sauce, if desired.

Choose Your Own Frittata

Frittatas are customisable with just about anything you have on hand. Use leftover vegetables, change up the cheese (or use two different kinds!), or add a breakfast protein if that's what your household desires.

Round out the meal with some crusty bread and a green salad dressed with a citrusy vinaigrette.

Owl

'Please, no interruptions.'

Wise and learned Owl remains always ready to offer tremendous insight gleaned from his many books (as best as he can recall). Being Owl is a bird of such informed taste, it may be enlightening to read up on his sophisticated menu for yourself.

RECIPES:

Smoked Trout Dip . . . . page 63

Grilled Asparagus with
Green Goddess Dressing . . . . . page 79

Pizzelle Snowflakes . . . . page 115

Grilled Salmon with
Honey-Coriander Glaze . . . . . page 140

Za'atar Roasted Chickpeas, Butternut Squash, and Red Onions with Lime Yoghurt

A delicious supper can also be the prize at the end of a day. For instance, after Winnie the Pooh (again) became stuck in a hole just a bit too small for his after-lunch tummy. Though not in Rabbit's home this time (thankfully), Pooh Bear was instead in the garden. Fortunately, the friendly Gopher happened to be whistling by at the moment. (Very fortunate to catch him because, as he will remind you, he's not in the book.) None could lift a rather full Winnie the Pooh, but Gopher could instead dig a much more favourable opening. Rabbit was so grateful and relieved to not have to prune and water Pooh that he sent Gopher home with a great reward of squashes, chickpeas, onions, and other delights.

Though we have no way to know what Gopher prepared (as he is not in the book), one hopes he made as dynamic and flavourful a supper as this. Roasted chickpeas take on a crisp texture and absorb the dynamic, complex seasoning. The melty, rich butternut squash and earthy, sweet roasted red onion create a complement in texture and tone. Topping the warm mix with cool, tart, lime-zested yoghurt proves hard work can be its own reward.

YIELD: 4 servings

- One 450-gram can chickpeas
- 1 medium butternut squash (about 680 grams)
- 1 large red onion (about 340 grams)
- 45 millilitres extra-virgin olive oil
- 6 grams za'atar spice blend (see Ingredients and Methods, page 168)
- Kosher (coarse) salt
- Freshly ground black pepper
- 240 grams natural Greek yoghurt
- 45 millilitres water
- 1 gram freshly grated lime zest

Arrange an oven shelf to the second-from-the-top position and preheat the oven to 220°C, or gas mark 7.

Drain and rinse the chickpeas. Dump them onto a clean tea towel or several sheets of paper and pat them as dry as you can. It's OK that some of the skins will loosen. You can pick them out or leave them be.

Peel the squash and cut it in half lengthways. Scrape out the seeds (a grapefruit spoon works great for this). Cut the squash crosswise into about 12-millimetre-thick slices. Halve and peel the onion. Trim the hairy part of the root end but leave the root intact. Cut 2-centimetre wedges through the root end.

On a baking tray, toss the chickpeas, squash, and onion with the olive oil, za'atar, 1.65 grams of salt, and pepper to taste. Spread out evenly and arrange so the flat sides of the squash and onion touch the pan. Roast until the squash is tender and golden brown and the chickpeas and onion are wrinkled and soft, about 30 minutes.

Meanwhile, in a small bowl, stir together the yoghurt, water, lime zest, and a pinch of salt.

Transfer the chickpeas and vegetables to a serving bowl. Serve with the yoghurt drizzled over top.

Sweetcorn and Potato Chowder

For an anxious little creature like Piglet, the promise of a supper is to return home safe and sound with a comforting meal to help soothe the day's worries. And few choices are as instantly calming and fortifying as a warm bowl of soup. From the first sniff in your snout of this creamy blend of hearty potatoes and sweetcorn enriched with sautéed garlic and onions, you can breathe easier and enjoy your calming reward for once again braving the world.

YIELD: 4 servings (475 millilitres per person)

56 grams unsalted butter

4 thick spring onions, chopped, white and light green parts kept separate from the dark green parts

2 cloves garlic, finely grated

2 large russet potatoes, peeled and cut into 2-centimetre cubes (about 570 grams)

465 grams sweetcorn kernels, thawed if frozen

1.6 grams fresh thyme leaves

950 millilitres low-sodium vegetable stock, plus more as needed

Kosher (coarse) salt

Freshly ground black pepper

240 millilitres milk

SPECIAL TOOL
Blender

In a large soup pot, melt the butter over a medium heat. Once it starts to sizzle, add the white and light green parts of the spring onions and the garlic and cook, stirring occasionally, until the garlic is light golden and the spring onions are soft, about 3 minutes. Add the potatoes, sweetcorn, and thyme and pour in the stock, making sure the potatoes are just covered (add more stock or water as needed). Season with 7 grams salt and pepper to taste. Raise the heat and bring the liquid to a simmer and simmer until the potatoes are cooked through, about 12 minutes.

Transfer about 475 millilitres of the chowder to a blender. With the lid slightly ajar and covered with a clean tea towel, purée the chowder. Return the purée to the pan and stir to combine. Add the milk and cook to warm through, a few more minutes. Season with salt and pepper as needed.

Divide the chowder amongst bowls and garnish with the dark green parts of the spring onions.

Fusilli Pasta with Pistachio Pesto and Peas

When learning facts about donkeys, one might find they spend much of their days out and about, grazing on greens of all sorts. But knowing facts about things is hardly the same as knowing something yourself, and Winnie the Pooh knew for himself that Eeyore (the donkey) many days simply did not have the spirit to be out or about. (Let alone grazing, for that matter.) On some of those days, Pooh Bear would arrange for friends to bring the grazing to Eeyore.

One meal that brings such a bright sensation to the table is this pesto pasta with (equally) green peas. The satisfying noodles capture all the dynamic garlic and nutty flavours of the pesto. Peas and parsley add pops of light freshness, with a touch of lemon zest for a taste of sunshine.

YIELD: 4 servings

128 grams fresh flat-leaf parsley, leaves and tender stems only

2 cloves garlic, smashed

57.5 grams roasted pistachios

120 millilitres extra-virgin olive oil

57.5 grams finely grated Parmesan cheese, plus more for serving, as desired

Kosher (coarse) salt

450 grams fusilli pasta

140 grams petite peas, thawed if frozen

Freshly grated lemon zest, for serving

SPECIAL TOOL
Food processor

In a food processor, blend the parsley, garlic, and pistachios until the nuts are finely chopped. With the motor running, add the oil in a steady stream until the pesto comes together, scraping the bowl as needed. Transfer to a bowl. Stir in the Parmesan cheese and 0.8 gram of salt. (Makes about 240 grams.)

Bring a large pot of well-salted water to the boil over a high heat. Add the fusilli and cook according to the package directions. Reserve 240 millilitres of the pasta cooking water. Drain the pasta and return to the pot. Stir in about 180 grams of the pesto along with enough pasta water to create a sauce that clings to the pasta. Stir in the peas until warmed through.

Divide the pasta amongst plates, and top with the lemon zest (and more cheese, if desired).

NOTE: *There is more pesto than needed for the fusilli. It can easily be frozen in small quantities for future pasta dishes.*

Suppers 137

Chilli Cornbread Casserole

Though it has been proven that tiggers are tremendously picky eaters, preferring Essence of Malt above all else (despite insisting they like *everything* except honey, and haycorns, and thistles, and everything in the cupboard), our very own Tigger will, on some Occasions, have a few spoonfuls of a proper meal for 'strengthening.' On such an Occasion, it is best to prepare a meal that offers a rich variety of nutritional elements in each scoop. This hearty casserole layers sweet and satisfying cornbread over a blend of turkey, tomato, cheese, and enough dynamic spices to invigorate in every bite. For extra encouragement, the dish can be finished to a *T* for *Tigger*, as the one thing tiggers enjoy more than Essence of Malt is tiggers themselves.

YIELD: 4 to 6 servings

- 30 millilitres neutral oil, divided
- 450 grams minced turkey
- 2.5 grams kosher (coarse) salt, divided
- Freshly ground black pepper
- 1 small onion, chopped (about 80 grams)
- 3 cloves garlic, minced
- 16 grams tomato purée
- 5 grams chilli powder
- One 425-gram can crushed tomatoes
- One 240-gram box cornbread mix
- 115 grams Monterey jack cheese, grated
- ½ red jalapeño, halved lengthways, seeded, and cut crosswise into thin slices

NOTE: *Don't like the heat? Use red peppers instead!*

Preheat the oven to 200°C, or gas mark 6.

In a 30-centimetre ovenproof frying pan, heat 15 millilitres of oil over medium-high heat. Add the turkey, 1.65 grams of salt, and black pepper to taste and cook until cooked through, breaking the meat up with a wooden spoon, 5 to 6 minutes. Drain any liquid and transfer the turkey to a bowl. Heat the remaining 15 millilitres of oil in the frying pan and add the onion and garlic and cook until soft, adjusting the heat if sticking or browning too quickly, about 4 minutes. Stir in the tomato purée for about 30 seconds to coat the onion. Return the turkey to the pan and add the chilli powder and the remaining 0.85 gram of salt. Add the crushed tomatoes and stir to warm through. Turn off the heat.

In a medium bowl, prepare the cornbread mix according to the package directions.

Evenly scatter the cheese over the top of the chilli. Dollop the cornbread batter on top of the cheese and use a spatula to smooth the top. Arrange the jalapeño slices in a T shape, with the cut sides lightly pressed into the batter. Bake until the cornbread is golden brown and the turkey filling is bubbling at the edges, about 20 minutes. Let the casserole sit for at least 10 minutes before serving.

Grilled Salmon with Honey-Coriander Glaze

Choosing the perfect menu for a supper, of course, depends entirely on whose appetite needs to be satiated. When guests may seem as different as, say, wise old Owl and Winnie the Pooh (who attests to being a Bear of Very Little Brain), finding common ground may seem impossible. But a perfect dish is always one that unites separate tastes into a wonderful shared experience.

Here, rich and succulent salmon (a favourite of birds of prey and bears alike) is enriched with the sophisticated sharp and lemony tones of coriander and the simple sweetness of honey.

YIELD: 4 servings

5 grams coriander seeds, toasted (see Ingredients and Methods, page 168), or ground coriander

80 grams honey

11.65 grams kosher (coarse) salt, divided

Four 140- to 170-gram boneless, skinless centre-cut salmon fillets (about 2.5 centimetres thick), patted dry

Neutral oil, for brushing

Freshly ground black pepper

SPECIAL TOOL
Mortar and pestle

In a pestle, use a mortar to grind the coriander into a coarse powder. In a small bowl, stir together the coriander, honey, and 1.65 grams of salt. The mixture will be thick. You can warm the honey just a touch, but it will slide off the fish if it's too warm. Set aside.

Set an oven shelf to about 15 centimetres below the grill element and preheat the grill to high. Line a baking tray with foil. Place the salmon fillets on the pan, brush all sides lightly with oil, then season all over with the remaining 10 grams of salt and pepper to taste. (If one end of the fillet is very thin, partially tuck it underneath to even out the thickness.) Arrange the fillets skin sides down. Grill the salmon until lightly golden and an instant-read thermometer inserted in the thickest part of the fillet registers 51.6°C (for medium-rare), about 5 minutes.

NOTE: *Grills in electric ovens cycle on and off. Make sure the grill element is red hot before putting the salmon into the oven.*

Plate the salmon and spoon the honey-coriander glaze over the fillets. Let the heat of the salmon loosen the glaze, then brush it all over the top and sides.

Don't Fear the Salmon Skin

- If your salmon still has its skin, you can leave it on while cooking. Once cooked, run a fish spatula or metal turner between the skin and fillet and lift it off the fish.

- To identify the skin side of a skinless salmon fillet, look for the side with a greyish-brown layer. That's the fat between the skin and the flesh.

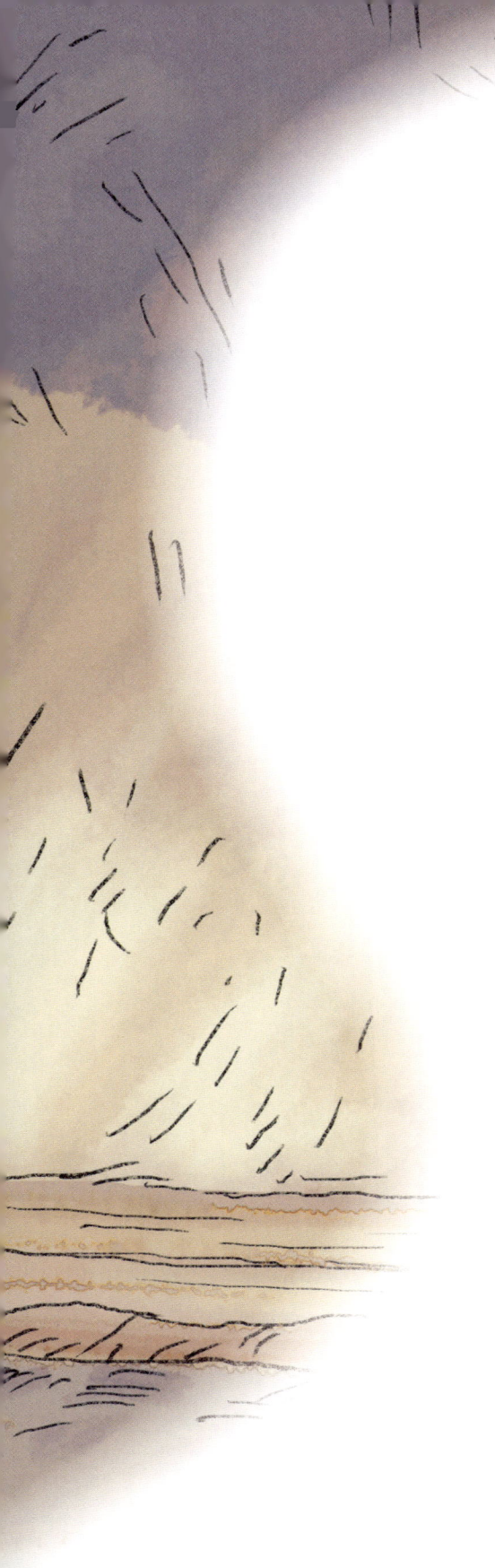

Chapter 6

Smackerels

A tummy does not wait until a mealtime to rumble. (Certainly not the tummy belonging to Winnie the Pooh.)

Pooh Bear himself noticed a reliable grumble for honey each morning around eleven. When the clock in his home stopped at ten fifty-five, he hardly noticed. Instead, whenever he saw it, he thought something to the effect of 'Oh dear, it's almost eleven. I should have a little smackerel of something.' And, in fact, no matter what time of day it really was, he was all the happier for it.

So perhaps we can learn from Pooh. It may be wise to have a few smaller morsels ready that you may prepare whenever you get that 'eleven o'clock feeling.' These final recipes hope to help across a variety of occasions and cravings—to quiet those rumblings in a most delightful way.

Piglet's Big Goat's Cheese Log

Throughout the Hundred-Acre Wood, there is no shortage of fallen logs. Though Christopher Robin readily enjoys them as items for climbing, hopping, and balancing, to poor Piglet, they are troubling reminders that Trees Sometimes Fall. And, being surrounded by trees in those moments, the reminder was a frightening sort of thought that took him out of the climbing, hopping, and balancing spirit.

A simple solution may be found in this savoury, aromatically seasoned snack. When fully prepared and coated with assorted herbs and crushed nuts, a rich goat's cheese log begins to look a great deal like the fallen, mossy sort. However, this small (and therefore hardly intimidating) delight is so unforgettably zesty and satisfying that, soon, the sight of toppled trees (of any size) will evoke memories of hearty cream, the crunch of earthy nuts, and notes of fresh rosemary and chives spread across your favourite savoury biscuit. Then, rather than feeling scared, even the smallest piglets will have a sudden urge for this goat's cheese log.

YIELD: 6 servings

- 12 grams chopped fresh chives
- 0.6 gram minced fresh rosemary
- 70 grams whole almonds, chopped
- One 300-gram log soft goat's cheese
- Savoury biscuits, for serving

On a large plate, mix together the chives, rosemary, and almonds. Gently press the goat's cheese log into the mixture and turn to coat, pressing to adhere the herbs and nuts to the cheese. If the nuts aren't sticking to the cheese, allow the cheese to soften a bit.

Serve with savoury biscuits.

> **Choose Your Own Toppings**
>
> Don't like almonds? Swap them out with your favourite nut. A combination of nuts would also work well.
>
> The same goes for the herbs, of course!

Smackerels 145

Pimiento Cheese Toasties

Though little ones like Roo may only require little smackerels when hungry, they usually like it best when the food is simple and fun (and maybe even a bit messy). The 'simple' comes in starting with a child favourite: the toasted cheese sandwich. The fun (and perhaps a bit of a mess) comes when you stuff it full of melting cheddar, an extra slather of soft cream cheese, and the sweet zing of pimiento red peppers. When this rich, gooey blend of creamy, zesty flavour is thick between buttery, toasted sourdough bread, this kid-friendly snack is sophisticated enough to appeal to momma Kanga's tastes, too.

YIELD: 4 servings

225 grams sharp cheddar cheese

30 grams soft cream cheese

130 grams chopped pimientos or (90 grams) roasted red peppers

Mayonnaise or room-temperature unsalted butter, for toasting

8 slices soureddough sandwich bread

SPECIAL TOOL
Food processor

Shred the cheddar cheese on the large holes of a box grater (or put through the shredder attachment on a food processor). In a food processor, combine the cheddar cheese, soft cream cheese, and pimientos. Pulse until combined but not a paste.

Spread the mayonnaise on one side of two slices of bread. Place the mayonnaise side down in a 30-centimetre non-stick frying pan and spread a quarter of the pimiento cheese (about 93 grams) on top of each slice. Spread the mayonnaise on two more slices of bread and place mayonnaise side up on top of the cheese. Turn the heat to medium-low and slowly begin to toast the sandwiches, adjusting the heat as needed. When they're toasted on the first side, after about 15 minutes, flip and continue toasting until the second side is done, 4 to 5 more minutes, adjusting the heat as needed to prevent burning.

Repeat with the remaining bread, mayo, and pimiento cheese to make two more sandwiches.

More Cheese, Please

These sandwiches were originally made with square sourdough bread slices. If you can only find sourdough in a boule shape, to fill the larger bread slices, you may need to make more pimiento cheese, which is never a bad thing.

Crumpet Antipasti Pizza

After several pages without a mention, it is most likely Eeyore is slumping down somewhere in the Wood quietly mumbling, 'I bet they forgot about me again, didn't they.' So it will just as likely be a happy surprise when he tastes these savoury little snacks you were about to make, with him in mind!

Much like Eeyore, the simple but hearty crumpets allow the other ingredients to get the glory: tangy marinara, creamy mozzarella, and spiky, earthy artichokes (a more suitable substitute for his favourite thistles). To better fit our forlorn friend, add salty black olives and soured pepperoncini, balanced with the softly sweet roasted red peppers.

YIELD: 6 servings

- 6 crumpets, split
- 120 to 180 millilitres marinara sauce
- 90 to 115 grams shredded mozzarella
- About 32 grams sliced black olives or your favourite olive
- About 90 grams chopped roasted red peppers
- 6 pepperoncini, sliced
- 12 marinated artichoke quarters
- Grated Parmesan cheese, for sprinkling

Arrange an oven shelf to the second position from the top (about 15 centimetres away from the grill element). Preheat the grill to high.

Put the crumpets on a baking tray. Broil until toasted to your liking, 2 to 3 minutes.

On each muffin half, spread 15 to 30 millilitres of marinara sauce, top with 15 to 23 grams of cheese, then top with assorted toppings as desired. Grill until the cheese is melted, keeping an eye on the pizzas the whole time, about 2 minutes. Sprinkle with grated Parmesan before serving.

Fresh Cabbage Pancakes

To Rabbit, every guest's rumbling for an afternoon snack becomes an opportunity to convince friends to share his love of vegetables. In particular, perhaps no vegetable is as unjustly dismissed as his beloved cabbage.

If you, yourself, just wrinkled your nose at the thought of a cabbage dish, have compassion for Rabbit and give this surprising, winning preparation a try. Crispy fried onions and tender spring onions give these small, snacky, savoury pancakes a sweet, mild onion flavour, whereas the ginger adds a bit of zest. The hoisin mayo is creamy, tangy, and sweet.

YIELD: 4 servings (8 pancakes)

HOISIN MAYO
- 120 grams mayonnaise
- 10 grams hoisin sauce (see Ingredients and Methods, page 168)
- 5 millilitres freshly squeezed lemon juice
- 2.5 millilitres toasted sesame oil

PANCAKES
- 60 grams plain flour
- 1.65 grams kosher (coarse) salt
- 1.15 grams baking powder
- 1 gram sugar
- 2 large eggs
- 60 millilitres low-sodium chicken broth
- 1.85 grams finely grated peeled fresh ginger (from about a 2.5-by-2.5-centimetre knob)
- 2 spring onions, thinly sliced on the diagonal, plus more for garnish
- ½ head green cabbage (about 225 grams), cored and chopped into 6-millimetre pieces
- 14 grams crispy french fried onions, lightly crushed, plus more for garnish
- Neutral oil, for frying

SPECIAL TOOL
Thin flexible spatula (like a fish spatula)

To make the hoisin mayo: In a small bowl, whisk together the mayonnaise, hoisin sauce, lemon juice, and sesame oil. Set aside.

To make the pancakes: In a large bowl, whisk together the flour, salt, baking powder, and sugar. In a medium bowl, whisk the eggs, broth, and ginger. Pour the egg mixture into the flour mixture, add the spring onions, and whisk until well combined. Fold in the cabbage and fried onions. The mixture will look like chopped cabbage barely bound by batter.

In a large non-stick frying pan over medium heat, heat 60 millilitres oil until hot, 4 to 5 minutes. Scoop 60 millilitres of the cabbage mixture into the pan and spread into a 7.5-centimetre-wide pancake. Make more pancakes in the pan without crowding the pan. Cook until the bottoms of the pancakes are golden brown, about 4 minutes. Flip the pancakes without pressing down (or the pancakes will be dense). Cook until the other side is golden brown, about 3 minutes. Transfer the pancakes to a wire rack as they're done. Continue making pancakes with the remaining cabbage mixture, adding more oil as needed.

Serve the pancakes slathered with some hoisin mayo and sprinkled with the reserved spring onions and fried onions.

Pooh's Pasties

The quintessentially English smackerel, the meat pie, may be lightly redressed to commemorate perhaps the most quintessential tale of the Hundred-Acre Wood, when Winnie the Pooh became stuck in Rabbit's front door. As well-known as any (mis?)adventures here, its great retelling may be due to the sheer number of friends and relations called to help. Just as Rabbit turned his back-end view into home decor, some additional decorative pastry shapes re-create that same sight. The resulting savoury treats make a poetic, homemade thank-you gift for any friends who have helped you out of jam.

YIELD: 4 pasties

225 grams minced turkey, preferably dark meat

16 grams fresh flat-leaf parsley leaves, chopped

15 millilitres Worcestershire sauce

4 grams kosher (coarse) salt

Freshly ground black pepper

½ medium Yukon Gold or other yellow potato, cut into 1-centimetre dice (about 83 grams)

½ small onion, cut into 6-millimetre dice (about 55 grams)

80 grams frozen peas and carrots mix

28 grams unsalted butter, cut into small bits

Plain flour, for dusting

One 399.7-gram box store-bought refrigerated piecrusts, at room temperature (see Ingredients and Methods, page 168)

1 large egg, beaten with a splash of water

SPECIAL TOOLS

5-centimetre, 10-centimetre, and 12-centimetre round biscuit cutters

2.5-centimetre mini Christmas stocking biscuit cutter (optional)

Or handmade templates of the biscuit cutters (see Ingredients and Methods, page 168)

Pie-Making Tips

- When cutting the dough, position the circles close to each other to maximise the space for the other cutouts.
- You can make these pasties vegetarian by swapping the meat with swede or more potatoes and peas and carrots.

Preheat the oven to 190°C, or gas mark 5. Line a baking tray with baking paper.

In a large and wide shallow bowl, gently combine the turkey, parsley, Worcestershire sauce, salt, and pepper to taste. Top with the potato, onion, frozen peas and carrots, and butter and gently mix. Set aside.

Dust a work surface with flour. Unfold and roll one piecrust to 3 millimetres thick. Cut out four 10-centimetre circles. Unfold and roll the other piecrust and cut into four 12-centimetre circles. Roll each 12-centimetre circle into a 13-centimetre circle. With the remaining scraps of dough, cut out four 5-centimetre circles and eight Pooh legs.

Brush the edge of one 10-centimetre dough circle with the egg wash. Mound one-quarter of the filling in the middle of the circle, leaving about a 6-millimetre border. Top with a 13-centimetre dough circle and gently press the edges together. Crimp with the tines of a fork to seal. Brush all over with the egg wash. Centre a 5-centimetre dough circle on top of the crust and brush with egg wash. Attach the legs to the 5-centimetre circle and brush with egg wash. Make three more pasties with the remaining dough circles, legs, filling, and egg wash, transferring them to the prepared baking tray as done. Cut a few vents in each pasty to allow steam to escape.

Bake until the pasties are golden brown, 40 to 45 minutes. Let cool for 10 minutes before serving.

Tigger-Striped Biscuits

Of all the friends in the Hundred-Acre Wood, Tigger is the most likely to not be found when you look for him. After all, tiggers are so full of playfulness, they must spend a great deal of the day bouncing it out, so as to make room for tomorrow's portion. Fortunately, these Tigger-Striped Biscuits are like bringing a bit of our striped friend anywhere you go. These layered, crumbly delights pattern stripes of cocoa and orange-zest flavour onto sweet vanilla. When baked and sugared, they pounce with all the sweetness and energy of Tigger leaping to greet you.

YIELD: About 6 dozen biscuits

- 226 grams (2 sticks) unsalted butter, at room temperature
- 150 grams caster sugar
- 28 grams icing sugar
- 4 grams kosher (coarse) salt
- 2 large eggs, separated, whites lightly beaten, at room temperature
- 10 millilitres vanilla essence
- 280 to 300 grams plain flour, divided, plus more for dusting
- Freshly grated zest from 2 oranges
- Orange (or red and yellow) gel food colour, as needed
- 27 grams Dutch-process cocoa powder
- Demerara or coloured sanding sugar, for coating

In the bowl of a stand mixer fitted with the paddle attachment, beat the butter, caster and icing sugars, and salt on medium-high speed until the mixture is pale yellow and very fluffy, about 3 minutes. Scrape down the sides of the bowl. Add the egg yolks (reserving the whites) and vanilla and beat until smooth. Scrape down the sides of the bowl. Add 240 grams of flour and mix until incorporated.

Divide the dough into thirds, leaving two-thirds in the bowl. The remaining one-third will be for the cocoa dough. Add the orange zest and 40 grams of flour to the bowl and mix until tacky but not sticky. Remove one-third of the dough from the bowl and set aside as the white dough.

Add orange or a mix of red and yellow food colour to the dough in the bowl and mix until you have the desired shade of orange. Depending on the amount of food colour used, the dough may become too sticky. If so, mix in flour, 7.5 grams at a time, until the orange dough is the same consistency as the white dough. Remove the orange dough from the bowl and set aside.

Return the reserved dough for the cocoa dough to the bowl, add the cocoa powder, and mix until incorporated. Set aside.

Divide each colour of dough in half. On a lightly floured sheet of baking paper, roll half of the white dough into a 7.5-by-20-centimetre rectangle. Pat half of the orange dough on top of the white dough, followed by a layer of half of the chocolate

Continued on page 156

dough. Tiger stripes aren't perfectly even, so when stacking the dough layers, don't make the stripes perfectly flat. Let the layers be uneven and wavy and not completely spread to both edges of the biscuits. Repeat layering with the remaining orange and chocolate dough. On another sheet of lightly floured baking paper, roll the white dough to the dimensions of the stack (it will have spread from the patting) and transfer it onto the stack. Gently roll or flatten the stack into a 10-by-25-centimetre-wide rectangle. Don't press too hard or the stripes will flatten out. Cut the stacks in half lengthways and then crosswise into four bars. Slide the baking paper and bars onto a baking tray, then cover with another sheet of baking paper. Chill the bars until very firm but not frozen, about 1 hour in the freezer or 2 hours in the fridge.

Preheat the oven to 180°C, or gas mark 4. Line 3 baking trays with baking paper.

Put the demerara or sanding sugar in a wide, shallow bowl. Lightly brush one bar of dough with the egg whites, then roll it in the decorating sugar, pressing the sugar firmly onto the dough to adhere. Slice the bar crosswise into 6-millimetre-thick biscuits and arrange 4 centimetres apart on the prepared baking tray. Repeat with the other three bars of dough, egg whites, and sugar. Bake the biscuits, rotating the trays halfway through, until the white dough on the bottom of the biscuits is lightly browned, 13 to 15 minutes. Let the biscuits cool on the trays.

Reduce and Reuse

You can reuse the baking paper by lining your baking trays with the paper used for rolling out the dough.

Christopher Robin

'Silly old bear.'

The best friend a bear could ask for, Christopher Robin brings adventure, lessons about the world, and true kindness each time he comes to the Hundred-Acre Wood. A growing boy needs to stay well-fed, of course—so perhaps prepare one of these to celebrate his next return.

RECIPES:

Honey-Poached Pears . . . . page 37

Chocolate Bark with Pretzels
and Dried Cranberries . . . . page 99

Lemon Posset Glazed
with Marmalade. . . . . page 120

Mushrooms on Toast . . . . page 125

Haycorns

Little boys like Christopher Robin simply are not meant to eat haycorns. This is one way, at least, where the very small Piglet may be made of stronger stuff. But should you hear Piglet describe the taste he enjoys so greatly, one would suspect haycorns were almost impossibly delicious enough to risk tooth and jaw.

Instead, try these almost impossibly delicious, human-friendly Haycorns. Each (gentler) bite bursts with sweet, crunchy peanut butter enriched with butter and vanilla. When they're dipped in chocolate and chilled, you may feel compelled to gather your own stockpile of these nutty treats.

YIELD: About 15 haycorns

- 112 grams icing sugar, sifted
- 130 grams chunky peanut butter (not 'natural' style)
- 42 grams unsalted butter, melted
- 2.5 millilitres vanilla essence
- 0.8 gram kosher (coarse) salt
- 127.5 grams plain semisweet or milk chocolate morsels
- 4 grams vegetable lard or coconut oil

SPECIAL TOOLS
Electric whisk
Toothpicks

Line a baking tray with baking paper and set aside.

In a medium bowl, use an electic mixer on low speed to beat the icing sugar, peanut butter, butter, vanilla, and salt until well combined. Roll about 15 grams of the mixture between your palms and form a 3-centimetre-wide eggish shape. Place it on its side on the prepared baking tray. Repeat forming the acorns with the remaining peanut butter mixture. Freeze until they are firm, about 15 minutes.

Once the acorns have chilled, in a small microwave-safe bowl, microwave the chocolate morsels and vegetable lard or coconut oil in three or four 30-second intervals, stirring after each interval, until melted and smooth.

Skewer the wide end of an acorn with a toothpick. Dip the tip end of the acorn into the chocolate until half to two-thirds of the acorn is covered. (The uncovered peanut butter top will be the acorn cap.) Gently twirl the toothpick between your fingers so the excess chocolate drips off. Return the acorn to the baking tray and remove the toothpick. Repeat until all the acorns are coated, reheating the chocolate to loosen as necessary.

Pop the acorns back into the freezer for another 10 minutes. Use the tip of a toothpick to scratch crosshatch marks on the surface of the peanut butter to mimic an acorn cap. Dab some of the thickened chocolate on top where the toothpick hole is for a stem. Store the acorns in an airtight container in the fridge for two weeks or the freezer for up to two months.

Eyeore's Tails

You may have heard tale (not *T-A-I-L*) of the time poor Eeyore sadly discovered he had lost his tail (not *T-A-L-E*). His friends showed great compassion and put in great effort to find a suitable replacement. (That is, until Pooh managed to find Eeyore's actual tail, hung at Owl's door as a bellpull.)

So whether as a reward for Pooh, a comfort to Eeyore, or a batch of replacements for next time, these tasty tails can be easily made to match (and may be sticky enough to stay on). Classic gooey, marshmallowy crispy rice cereal treats are finished with Eeyore's signature bow made of tangy-sweet fruit leathers (and a freeze-dried blueberry 'tack') for a pop of extra fun flavour and texture.

YIELD: 16 tails

Non-stick cooking spray
140 grams mini marshmallows
56 grams unsalted butter, cut into pats
5 millilitres vanilla essence
Pinch kosher (coarse) salt
Blue and red gel food colour, as needed

NOTE: *Use gel food colour here. Liquid food colour will result in soggy treats.*

150 grams crispy rice cereal
Pink or red fruit leather in thin sheets, rolls, or tape form, for the bows
Ready-to-use chocolate-flavoured biscuit icing, for decorating
16 freeze-dried blueberries

Eeyore's Tail Replacements (Rejected)

Should our dear Eeyore once again lose his tail, know that the following have already been tried as replacements, but proved poorly suited:

- Balloon
- Cuckoo clock
- Yo-yo
- Umbrella
- Dartboard
- Party hat
- Wooden duck
- Moose décor
- Weathervane
- Accordion

Line the bottom and sides of an 20-by-20-centimetre oven baking dish with baking paper. Spray the paper, a rubber spatula, and a large microwave-safe bowl with cooking spray and set aside.

Put the marshmallows and butter in the prepared bowl and microwave, uncovered, until the marshmallows are puffy, about 1 minute. Add the vanilla, salt, and a mix of blue and red food colour to match Eeyore's bluish colouring. Mix with the spatula, adjusting the colour as necessary. Quickly stir in the cereal to coat evenly. Scrape the mixture into the prepared oven dish. With lightly oiled hands, press the cereal firmly into an even layer in the pan. Let the crispy rice treats cool, about 30 minutes.

Transfer the treats to a chopping board. Cut them into eight 2.5-centimetre-wide strips, then cut the strips in half crosswise to make sixteen 10-by-2.5-centimetre rectangles. Use your fingers to taper one of the short ends of each strip to shape the tip of the tuft of hair at the end of Eeyore's tail.

Make 16 small bows with the fruit leather. Working with one tail at a time, use the biscuit icing to draw in the tuft of fur, then press a bow at the top of the tuft to glue it on. Place a dot of icing at the opposite end of the tail to glue on a dried blueberry. Repeat with the remaining tails. Let the icing dry before serving.

Malted Ice-Cream Sundae with Mini Malted Mochi

It should be recognised that Tigger has been very patient throughout most of this endeavour, hardly making a mess and rarely insisting discussion be about him. Such remarkable restraint and humility (another wonderful quality about tiggers, he says) deserves a delicious reward.

This celebratory sundae goes beyond the usual scoops of chocolate ice cream and stripes of rich caramel topping to add Tigger's favourite flavour of malt in both sweet malt powder and crispy, chocolatey malted milk balls. More of the icing cream flavour is dusted on bits of mochi, the lightly sweet Japanese treats that are springy and surprising. (In suitably Tigger-ish fashion.)

YIELD: 4 servings

MOCHI
80 grams sweet (glutinous) rice flour (see Ingredients and Methods, page 168)
25 grams sugar
12 grams malted milk powder, plus more for dusting
Pinch kosher (coarse) salt
120 millilitres milk
5 millilitres vanilla essence
Cornflour, for dusting

SUNDAE
Chocolate ice cream, for serving
Caramel sauce, for topping
Malted milk balls, halved or coarsely chopped, for topping
Maraschino cherries, for topping

SPECIAL TOOLS
Silicone spatula
Pastry cutter or pizza wheel (optional)
Four sundae glasses (optional)

To make the mochi: In a microwave-safe 950-millilitre liquid measuring cup or medium bowl, whisk together the rice flour, sugar, malted milk powder, and salt. Whisk in the milk and vanilla until smooth. Cover with clingfilm or a microwave-safe lid and microwave for 1½ minutes. Uncover the cup (be careful of the hot steam), saving the clingfilm or lid. Use a silicone spatula to stir the stiff mixture. Cover again and zap for another minute. Uncover and stir the mixture again until smooth and stretchy—it will get chewier the more it's mixed.

Generously dust a chopping board with cornflour. Scrape the mochi onto the cornflour and dust with more cornflour. Let it cool just until it can be handled. Pat the warm mochi flat into a 12-millimetre-thick sheet. Using a pastry cutter, pizza wheel, or knife, cut the mochi into 12-millimetre squares. Pull the squares apart and toss in the cornflour to coat evenly so they don't stick together. Toss the mochi in a large sieve or colander and shake off the excess cornflour. When ready to serve, transfer the mochi to a bowl and toss with malted milk powder to coat.

To make the sundaes: In four sundae glasses or bowls, assemble the sundaes by layering scoops of ice cream, caramel sauce, malted milk balls, and lots of mochi. Top each sundae with a cherry and serve immediately.

About Mochi

If the sundaes aren't being served soon after the mochi are made, store the mochi in an airtight container with cornflour for up to two days in a cool room-temperature spot or up to five days in the fridge. To soften chilled mochi, heat it in the microwave (covered) in 5-second increments.

Kiwi and Strawberry Ice Lollies

Especially sunshiny days deserve little treats all their own. Away from the shade of gathered groves and towering trees, a cloudless summer day in the Hundred-Acre Wood can get very hot indeed. On those sorts of days, Roo makes a point to hop his way to Rabbit's garden (as sunny a spot as one can find). For, as Rabbit toils in the sweltering sun, all Roo need say is 'Sure is a hot one, isn't it?' and Rabbit will pause to think and say 'You're right, Roo. It is.'

Then Rabbit will think to take a break in the shade of his home and make some delicious, real fruit ice lollies (like these) to cool them both down. Strawberry and kiwi are a popular combination for their complementary yet unique sweet-tart flavours. Here, the addition of honey brightens their sweetness and (once fully frozen) transforms the fruit into a true icy treat.

YIELD: Ten 90-millilitre ice lollies

- 285 grams fresh strawberries, hulled and quartered
- 60 grams honey or 37.5 grams sugar, divided, plus more as needed
- 30 millilitres freshly squeezed lime juice, divided
- 0.4 gram kosher (coarse) salt, divided
- 5 kiwis (about 570 grams), peeled and chopped

SPECIAL TOOLS
Blender or mini food processor (optional)
Ten 90-millilitre ice lolly moulds
10 wooden ice lolly sticks (depending on the type of mould)

In a blender or mini food processor, blend the strawberries, 20 grams of honey, 15 millilitres of lime juice, and a pinch of salt into a purée. Taste and sweeten with more honey if you'd like. Pour the purée into a liquid measuring cup or bowl. Pour 30 millilitres of the purée into each ice lolly mould and put in the freezer to partially firm up, about 45 minutes.

Rinse out the blender or mini food processor and measuring cup. Blend the kiwi with the remaining 40 grams of honey, remaining 15 millilitres lime juice, and a pinch of salt. (Be careful not to overblend.) Taste and sweeten with more honey if you'd like. Pour the purée into the measuring cup. Pour 30 millilitres of the purée on top of the strawberry layer in each ice pop mould and insert the sticks. Return the ice lollies to the freezer until firm, at least 4 hours.

To unmould, run the moulds under warm water or dip the moulds in a bowl of warm water until the ice lollies loosen.

Tips for Success

- You'll need 300 millilitres of each purée for these ice lollies. If you have less, add some water. If you have extra, it's great added to a drink like lemonade or sparkling water.
- The amount of the honey needed will depend on the sweetness of the fruit. Don't be too shy when sweetening the ice lolly base, as the frozen lollies will taste less sweet than the fresh purée.
- A mini food processor will make a chunkier purée, giving you an ice lolly with more texture. A blender will make a smoother purée, but the kiwi can become bitter and turn brownish if overblended, especially if using a high-powered blender.

Avocado Milk Shake

Lest we forget, our friend Winnie the Pooh also has a fondness for the sweetness of condensed milk. So before we leave him, do one more kindness and prepare this simple but delightful drink (just to ensure he is getting more vitamins, to be well until you meet again). Hearty, creamy avocado and the rich sweetness of condensed milk combine with the cold chill of blended ice to become an indulgent shake Pooh's sweet tooth can delight in (with far more health benefits than a pot of honey).

YIELD: 4 servings (about 1.3 litres)

- 2 medium ripe avocados, preferably Hass, halved and pitted (about 310 grams)
- 300 millilitres whole milk, plus more as needed
- 310 grams sweetened condensed milk
- Pinch kosher (coarse) salt
- 240 to 360 grams ice cubes, divided

SPECIAL TOOL
Blender

Chill 4 glasses.

Scoop the avocados out of their skins in chunks and put into the jar of a blender. Add the milk, condensed milk, salt, and about 240 grams of ice. Blend on the smoothie setting or high speed until thick and smooth. Add the remaining 120 grams of ice and blend until cold. The shake will be very thick. Add more milk if you prefer a thinner shake. Pour into the glasses and serve.

Fun Facts

- Avocado milk shakes or smoothies sweetened with condensed milk are popular in Southeast Asia, particularly in Vietnam and Indonesia. One Indonesian version includes coffee and a drizzle of chocolate syrup (perhaps something for parents to try).
- This is the perfect way to use up ripe avocados that are on the verge of becoming overripe.

Ingredients and Methods

INGREDIENTS

CANDY MELTS
Lightly flavoured and found in a multitude of colours, confectionery candy melt coins are good for decorating because they melt easily and harden quickly to make a smooth coating. They are not the same as chocolate because no cocoa butter is added. If adding a little neutral oil, which helps keep the coating smooth, do so before you add any food colouring to avoid a water-based product not mixing with the oil-based one.

GUAVA PASTE
Sweet and tart and often served with cheese, guava paste is a stiff, dense block of thickened and sweetened guava purée. Look for it packaged as clingfilm-wrapped blocks or in flat round tins in the international or Latin aisle of supermarkets or at a Latin market.

HOISIN SAUCE
Hoisin sauce is a thick, sweet, and savoury Chinese sauce made of fermented soybeans flavoured with sugar, sesame, garlic, chillies, and other seasonings. It is used as a condiment or dipping sauce, a flavouring in stir-fries, or part of a glaze or marinade.

KOSHER (COARSE) SALT
The crystal size of kosher (coarse) salt differs depending on the brand used. Our measurements are for Diamond kosher (coarse) salt. Halve the amount if using Morton's coarse kosher (coarse) salt, table salt, or fine sea salt and then adjust to taste.

LEMON CURD
Lemon curd is a smooth, tart, and sweet spread used for filling or topping pastries and baked goods of all sorts. Made from lemons, sugar, eggs, and sometimes butter, it differs from jams, jellies, custards, or pie fillings.

NEUTRAL OIL
Neutral oil is a cooking oil with mild or no flavour and a high smoke point, making it suitable for baking, making salad dressing, sautéing, and deep frying. Some choices are avocado, corn, rapeseed, vegetable, grapeseed, and sunflower oil.

PIECRUST (STORE-BOUGHT REFRIGERATED)
Store-bought refrigerated piecrusts come as rolled circles of dough packaged in a box—don't confuse them with piecrust shells. Bring the dough to room temperature according to package directions before using. If the dough becomes very soft and floppy during assembly, pop the pastry in the freezer for about 10 minutes to firm up.

PUFF PASTRY
Frozen puff pastry needs to be completely thawed in the fridge (usually overnight) and *just* pliable enough to unfold without cracking before using. The pastry needs to be handled quickly before it becomes too soft to work with. At that point, the fat in

the pastry starts to melt, and you'll lose the wonderful layers formed when it puffs up. If the pastry starts to go limp, slide it onto a baking paper-lined baking tray and pop it in the fridge or freezer until it firms up but is still pliable, about 10 minutes. The assembled pastry should be chilled again before baking. Baking puff pastry at a high oven temperature will provide a higher rise. Bake the pastry until it's a deep golden brown. Pale, or even golden, puff pastry may be gummy and not completely cooked through in the centre. Don't throw out the scraps of puff pastry! Brush them with leftover egg wash, sprinkle with sugar, and bake until dark golden.

SUMAC

The decorative sumac bush sports dark purple berries that, when ground or crushed, turn into a fruity, astringent seasoning that complements any dish that would benefit from a citrus-like boost. It's used across many cuisines but most often associated with Middle Eastern foods. Look for it in well-stocked supermarkets or Middle Eastern markets. (Note: It is not the same as the poisonous sumac shrub, which grows white berries.)

SWEET (GLUTINOUS) RICE FLOUR

Sweet rice flour, aka glutinous rice flour, is made from short-grain sticky rice, aka glutinous rice. It should not be confused with regular rice flour, which can be made from long-, medium-, or short-grain rice. Despite the name, sweet rice flour does not contain gluten.

TAHINI

A creamy paste made from ground sesame seeds, tahini is an essential ingredient in hummus as well as many other traditional Middle Eastern dishes. The oils and solids separate like natural peanut butter, so if you store yours in the fridge, you may want to bring it to room temperature to make stirring easier.

ZA'ATAR

Za'atar is a Middle Eastern seasoning blend that varies by region and even families. Aside from the name of the blend, it's also the name of the herb that is a relative of oregano. Other ingredients typically include sesame seeds, sumac, and salt. It gives an earthy, tangy flavouring to dips, roasted meats and vegetables, and just about anything that could use a zippy upgrade.

METHODS

BISCUIT CUTTERS

If you don't have the biscuit cutters in the size and shapes needed, draw and then cut out templates from paper or cardboard. Use the tip of a small, sharp knife to trace along the edges of the template.

CLEANING MUSHROOMS

If you're working with a small number of mushrooms, use damp kitchen paper or a tea towel to wipe off the dirt. If you're working with a good amount of mushrooms, quickly dunk them in a bowl of cold water and swish them around to loosen any dirt. Lift the mushrooms with your hands and put them in a colander to drain. Don't pour them with the water from the bowl into the colander, or all the dirt you washed off will land right back on the mushrooms. Spread the mushrooms on a tea towel and pat very dry. For cremini and white button mushrooms, trim off the tough woody ends of the stems. For shiitake mushrooms, cut off the whole stems. Mushroom stems can be used when making stock.

EGG WASH

Beat a whole egg with a splash of water, milk, or cream. Use the egg wash to seal pastry or brush on top of pastry before baking to create a shiny glaze.

MEASURING HONEY

Honey in jars is measured by weight because it's too viscous to be measured by volume.

MIXING LARGE AMOUNTS

When mixing large amounts of ingredients that can break apart, like in our Creamy Potato Salad with Pickled Mustard Seeds and Spring Onions (page 64), or be overworked like the meat mixture in the Pooh's Pasties (page 153), it can be helpful to spread and layer the ingredients on a baking tray or wide shallow bowl before mixing. This allows for a more evenly distributed mixture without overmixing.

PIZZELLE MAKERS

Pizzelle makers are also known as pizzelle presses, pizzelle bakers, and pizzelle irons (which are used on a gas hob). Sizes of pizzelle vary: 13 centimetres (full-size), 10 centimetres (medium), and 7.5 centimetres. The intricate designs on the pizzelle plates also differ, although snowflakes are classic.

TOASTING NUTS

Toasting (or roasting) nuts brings out their flavour and crisps them up. Preheat the oven to 180°C, or gas mark 4. Spread the nuts in a single layer on a baking tray. Roast, stirring occasionally, until the nuts are golden and nutty smelling, 6 to 8 minutes. Set aside to let cool.

TOASTING SPICES, SESAME SEEDS, AND PINE NUTS

Toasting whole spices, seeds, and small nuts brings out their aromatic oils, allowing their full flavour to shine. Put the spices, seeds, or nuts in a heavy frying pan over medium heat. Toast, shaking the pan often, until the spices are fragrant and lightly golden. When more than one spice in a recipe needs to be toasted, toast them separately, as they may require different toasting times. Let the spices cool before using.

WHIPPING CREAM

Make sure you're using chilled double cream (and if you'd like, especially if it's a hot day, chill your bowl and beaters as well). Starting at a low to medium-low speed with an electric whisk or stand mixer, whip the cream (there may be some splashing) until it starts to go from loose bubbles to a thicker consistency. You can toggle between speeds to find the sweet spot, but you don't want to beat it too much or the cream will turn into butter. You'll know it's ready when the peaks hold their shape but with a little droop at the top. It's best used freshly whipped, but it can also be stored covered in the fridge for a couple of hours.

About the Authors

Vivian Jao is a food writer, recipe developer and tester, food stylist, culinary producer, and culinary researcher based in the New York City area. A former director of the test kitchen at *Saveur* and columnist for *Every Day with Rachael Ray*, Vivian has also had her work appear in outlets including the Emmy-nominated show *The Kitchen*, *Bon Appétit*, Simply Recipes, *Taste of Home*, the *Wall Street Journal*, *Weight Watchers*, and *Prevention*. Vivian is a co-author of Judy Joo's *Korean Food Made Simple*. She has contributed to *The MeatEater Fish and Game Cookbook*, *Food Network Kitchens Cookbook*, *Edible Jersey Farmers' Markets Cookbook*, and more. Vivian is an IACP Awards Finalist for both Instructional Writing and Best Group Food Blog.

Liz Tarpy has been working in various food and recipe development roles for more than twenty-five years. She is a former employee of the Food Network, where she worked in the test kitchen, production kitchen, and editorial departments. She has contributed to various books and had her work run in many media outlets, with highlights including *The MeatEater Fish and Game Cookbook*, *Saveur*, and the anthology *Storied Dishes*.

James Asmus is a writer of books and comics as well as for theater, video games, and TV. His work in comic books has been nominated for several Harvey Awards and includes all-ages favorites such as The Amazing Spider-Man, My Little Pony, and Transformers: Bumblebee series. With Insight Editions, James has contributed to recipe books for Marvel's *Wolverine*, *Rick and Morty*, and *Supernatural* and is the author of *The Wisdom of Pooh* guided journal. James lives outside Portland, Oregon, with his wife and two weirdly wonderful kids.

Dedications

James
My work on this book is dedicated with love and honey to Irie, and her buddy Eeyore.

Vivian
Ben and Xavier, thank you for always being honest with your food critiques.

Liz
Mom, Joe, and Sandy, I wish you all could have seen this book.

Index

A
Acorn Squash, Smoked Paprika Baked, 86
almonds
    Green Couscous, 76
    Orange and Almond Scones with Honey Butter, 26
    Piglet's Big Goat's Cheese Log, 145
Apple Cupcakes, Honey, with Honey Soft Cream Cheese Frosting, 33
apricots, soft
    Coronation Chicken Sliders, 60
    Honey Nut Granola, 25
artichokes
    Crumpet Antipasti Pizza, 149
    Eeyore's 'Thistle' Soup, 109
asparagus
    Asparagus, Potato, and Pecorino Frittata, 129
    Grilled Asparagus with Green Goddess Dressing, 79
avocados
    Avocado Milk Shake, 166
    Cucumber, Dill, and Avocado Pressed Rice Sandwiches, 55

B
Baklava, Walnut, 30
barley
    Haycorn Tea, 59
basil
    Salted Watermelon Punch with Cucumber and Basil, 67
    Tomato and Herbed Ricotta Galette, 83
Basque Cheesecake with Orange Blossom Honey, 103
Beetroot-Dyed Deviled Eggs, 101
berries
    Dirt Cake Trifle, 47
    Eeyore's Tails, 161
    Hero Cake, 43
    Kiwi and Strawberry Ice Lollies, 165
    Pooh Bear Pancakes with Honey-Berry Compote, 15
    Rabbit's Smoothie, 93
biscuits
    Pizzelle Snowflakes, 115
    Thumbprint Biscuits, 49
    Tigger-Striped Biscuits, 154
bread
    in Coronation Chicken Sliders, 60
    in Cucumber, Dill, and Avocado Pressed Rice Sandwiches, 60
    in Eeyore's 'Thistle' Soup, 109
    in Mushrooms on Toast, 125
    in Open-Faced Radish and Herbed Cheese Tea Sandwiches, 52
    in Pimiento Cheese Toasties, 146
    in Stilton Toasts with Roasted Grapes, 110
butter
    Corn on the Cob with Whipped Honey-Miso Butter, 29
    Orange and Almond Scones with Honey Butter, 26
    Roasted Vegetable Platter with Honey Butter Glaze, 119
Butternut Squash, and Red Onions with Lime Yoghurt, Za'atar Roasted Chickpeas, 133

C
Cabbage Pancakes, Fresh, 150
cakes
    Basque Cheesecake with Orange Blossom Honey, 103
    Dirt Cake Trifle, 47
    Hero Cake, 43
carrots
    Pooh's Pasties, 153
    Roasted Vegetable Platter with Honey Butter Glaze, 119
    Veggie Chilli-Stuffed Jacket Potatoes, 89
Carrot-Ginger Dressing, Wedge Salad with, 71
Cauliflower Cheese with Pretzel Crust, 113
Celery Salad with Grainy Mustard Dressing, Smashed, 75
cheese. See also soft cream cheese
    Asparagus, Potato, and Pecorino Frittata, 129
    Cauliflower Cheese with Pretzel Crust, 113
    Cheese and Onion Pie, 126
    Chilli Cornbread Casserole, 139
    Crumpet Antipasti Pizza, 149
    Fusilli Pasta with Pistachio Pesto and Peas, 137
    Open-Faced Radish and Herbed Cheese Tea Sandwiches, 52
    Piglet's Big Goat's Cheese Log, 145
    Pimiento Cheese Toasties, 146
    Stilton Toasts with Roasted Grapes, 110
Cheese and Onion Pie, 126
Chicken Sliders, Coronation, 60
chickpeas
    Eeyore's Rainbow Veggie and Hummus Tray, 80
    Za'atar Roasted Chickpeas, Butternut Squash, and Red Onions with Lime Yoghurt, 133
Chilli Cornbread Casserole, 139
Chilli-Stuffed Jacket Potatoes, Veggie, 89
chives
    Coronation Chicken Sliders, 60
    Eeyore's 'Thistle' Soup, 109
    Grilled Asparagus with Green Goddess Dressing, 79
    Piglet's Big Goat's Cheese Log, 145
    Tomato and Herbed Ricotta Galette, 83
chocolate
    Chocolate Bark with Pretzels and Dried Cranberries, 99
    Chocolate-Dipped Honeycomb Sweets, 17
    Haycorns, 158
    Hero Cake, 43
    Tigger-Striped Biscuits, 154
Compote, Honey-Berry, 15
Coriander Glaze, Honey-, Grilled Salmon with, 140
Cornbread Casserole, Chilli, 139
Coronation Chicken Sliders, 60
courgette
    Trio of Quick Pickles, 90
Couscous, Green, 76
Cranberries, Chocolate Bark with Pretzels and Dried, 99
Creamy Potato Salad with Pickled Mustard Seeds and Spring Onions, 64
Crumpet Antipasti Pizza, 149
cucumbers
    Cucumber, Dill, and Avocado Pressed Rice Sandwiches, 55
    Salted Watermelon Punch with Cucumber and Basil, 67
    Wedge Salad with Carrot-Ginger Dressing, 71
Cupcakes, Honey Apple, with Honey Soft Cream Cheese Frosting, 33

D
dill
    Cucumber, Dill, and Avocado Pressed Rice Sandwiches, 55
    Trio of Quick Pickles, 90
dips and spreads
    Piglet's Big Goat's Cheese Log, 145
    Smoked Trout Dip, 63
Dirt Cake Trifle, 47
drinks
    Avocado Milk Shake, 166
    Haycorn Tea, 59
    Honey Lemonade with Mint Ice Cubes, 38

Rabbit's Smoothie, 93
Salted Watermelon Punch with Cucumber and Basil, 67
Witches' Brew, 106

E
Eeyore's Rainbow Veggie and Hummus Tray, 80
Eeyore's Tails, 161
Eeyore's 'Thistle' Soup, 109
eggs
    Asparagus, Potato, and Pecorino Frittata, 129
    Basque Cheesecake with Orange Blossom Honey, 103
    Beetroot-Dyed Deviled Eggs, 101

F
filo dough
    Walnut Baklava, 30
Fresh Cabbage Pancakes, 150
Frosting, Honey Soft Cream Cheese, 33
Fusilli Pasta with Pistachio Pesto and Peas, 137

G
Galette, Tomato and Herbed Ricotta, 83
Ginger Dressing, Carrot-, Wedge Salad with, 71
Granola, Honey Nut, 25
grapes
    Honeyed Yoghurt Parfait with Quinoa, Pomegranate Seeds, and Grapes, 22
    Stilton Toasts with Roasted Grapes, 110
Green Couscous, 76
Grilled Asparagus with Green Goddess Dressing, 79
Grilled Salmon with Honey-Coriander Glaze, 140
Guava and Soft Cream Cheese Hearts, 97

H
Haycorn Tea, 59
Haycorns, 158
Hero Cake, 43
honey
    Basque Cheesecake with Orange Blossom Honey, 103
    Chocolate-Dipped Honeycomb Sweets, 17
    Corn on the Cob with Whipped Honey-Miso Butter, 29
    Grilled Salmon with Honey-Coriander Glaze, 140
    Honey Apple Cupcakes with Honey Soft Cream Cheese Frosting, 33
    Honey Lemonade with Mint Ice Cubes, 38
    Honey Nut Granola, 25
    Honeyed Yoghurt Parfait with Quinoa, Pomegranate Seeds, and Grapes, 22
    Honey-Poached Pears, 37
    Kiwi and Strawberry Ice Lollies, 165
    Orange and Almond Scones with Honey Butter, 26
    Pooh Bear Pancakes with Honey-Berry Compote, 15
    Roasted Vegetable Platter with Honey Butter Glaze, 119
    Trio of Flavoured Honeys, 21
    Walnut Baklava, 30
Hummus Tray, Eeyore's Rainbow Veggie and, 80

I
Ice-Cream Sunday, Malted, with Mini Malted Mochi, 162
Ice Lollies, Kiwi and Strawberry, 165

K
Kiwi and Strawberry Ice Lollies, 165

L
lemons
    Honey Lemonade with Mint Ice Cubes, 38
    Lemon Posset Glazed with Marmalade, 120
Lime Yoghurt, Za'atar Roasted Chickpeas, Butternut Squash, and Red Onions with, 133

M
Malted Ice-Cream Sundae with Mini Malted Mochi, 162
Marmalade, Lemon Posset Glazed with, 120
mayonnaise
    Beetroot-Dyed Deviled Eggs, 101
    Creamy Potato Salad with Pickled Mustard Seeds and Spring Onions, 64
    Fresh Cabbage Pancakes, 150
    Grilled Asparagus with Green Goddess Dressing, 79
Milk Shake, Avocado, 166
mint
    Green Couscous, 76
    Honey Lemonade with Mint Ice Cubes, 38
    Sugar Snap Peas, Watercress, and Mint Salad, 72
Miso Butter, Whipped Honey-, Corn on the Cob with, 29
Mochi, Mini Malted, Malted Ice-Cream Sundae with, 162
Mushrooms on Toast, 125
Mustard Dressing, Grainy, Smashed Celery Salad with, 75
Mustard Seeds, Pickled, and Spring Onions, Creamy Potato Salad with, 64

O
oats
    Honey Nut Granola, 25
onions
    Cheese and Onion Pie, 126
    Za'atar Roasted Chickpeas, Butternut Squash, and Red Onions with Lime Yoghurt, 133
Open-Faced Radish and Herbed Cheese Tea Sandwiches, 52
oranges
    Basque Cheesecake with Orange Blossom Honey, 103
    Orange and Almond Scones with Honey Butter, 26
    Tigger-Striped Biscuits, 154

P
pancakes
    Fresh Cabbage Pancakes, 150
    Pooh Bear Pancakes with Honey-Berry Compote, 15
    Paprika Baked Acorn Squash, Smoked, 86
parsley
    Fusilli Pasta with Pistachio Pesto and Peas, 137
    Green Couscous, 76
    Grilled Asparagus with Green Goddess Dressing, 79
    Mushrooms on Toast, 125
    Pooh's Pasties, 153
peanut butter
    Haycorns, 158
Pears, Honey-Poached, 37
peas
    Fusilli Pasta with Pistachio Pesto and Peas, 137
    Pooh's Pasties, 153
    Pesto, Pistachio, and Peas, Fusilli Pasta with, 137
Pickles, Trio of Quick, 90
pies
    Cheese and Onion Pie, 126
    Pooh's Pasties, 153
Piglet's Big Goat's Cheese Log, 145
Pimiento Cheese Toasties, 146
Pistachio Pesto and Peas, Fusilli Pasta with, 137
Pizza, Crumpet Antipasti, 149
Pizzelle Snowflakes, 115

Pomegranate Seeds, and Grapes, Honeyed Yoghurt Parfait with Quinoa, 22
Pooh Bear Pancakes with Honey-Berry Compote, 15
Pooh's Pasties, 153
Posset, Lemon, Glazed with Marmalade, 120
potatoes
- Asparagus, Potato, and Pecorino Frittata, 129
- Creamy Potato Salad with Pickled Mustard Seeds and Spring Onions, 64
- Pooh's Pasties, 153
- Sweetcorn and Potato Chowder, 134
- Veggie Chilli-Stuffed Jacket Potatoes, 89

pretzels
- Cauliflower Cheese with Pretzel Crust, 113
- Chocolate Bark with Pretzels and Dried Cranberries, 99

puff pastry
- Guava and Soft Cream Cheese Hearts, 97

Q
Quinoa, Pomegranate Seeds, and Grapes, Honeyed Yoghurt Parfait with, 22

R
Rabbit's Smoothie, 93
radishes
- Green Couscous, 76
- Open-Faced Radish and Herbed Cheese Tea Sandwiches, 52
- Trio of Quick Pickles, 90

red peppers
- Crumpet Antipasti Pizza, 149
- Eeyore's Rainbow Veggie and Hummus Tray, 80
- Pimiento Cheese Toasties, 146

Rice Sandwiches, Pressed, Cucumber, Dill, and Avocado, 55
Ricotta Galette, Tomato and Herbed, 83
Roasted Vegetable Platter with Honey Butter Glaze, 119
rocket
- Green Couscous, 76

rosemary
- Piglet's Big Goat's Cheese Log, 145
- Trio of Flavoured Honeys, 21

S
salads
- Creamy Potato Salad with Pickled Mustard Seeds and Spring Onions, 64
- Smashed Celery Salad with Grainy Mustard Dressing, 75
- Sugar Snap Peas, Watercress, and Mint Salad, 72
- Wedge Salad with Carrot-Ginger Dressing, 71

Salmon, Grilled, with Honey-Coriander Glaze, 140
Salted Watermelon Punch with Cucumber and Basil, 67
sandwiches
- Coronation Chicken Sliders, 60
- Cucumber, Dill, and Avocado Pressed Rice Sandwiches, 55
- Open-Faced Radish and Herbed Cheese Tea Sandwiches, 52
- Pimiento Cheese Toasties, 146

Scones, Orange and Almond, with Honey Butter, 26
Smashed Celery Salad with Grainy Mustard Dressing, 75
Smoked Paprika Baked Acorn Squash, 86
Smoked Trout Dip, 63
Smoothie, Rabbit's, 93
soft cream cheese
- Basque Cheesecake with Orange Blossom Honey, 103
- Guava and Soft Cream Cheese Hearts, 97
- Honey Apple Cupcakes with Honey Soft Cream Cheese Frosting, 33
- Pimiento Cheese Toasties, 146
- Smoked Trout Dip, 63

soups
- Eeyore's 'Thistle' Soup, 109
- Sweetcorn and Potato Chowder, 134

soured cream
- Beetroot-Dyed Deviled Eggs, 101
- Grilled Asparagus with Green Goddess Dressing, 79
- Smoked Trout Dip, 63

spinach
- Rabbit's Smoothie, 93

spring onions
- Creamy Potato Salad with Pickled Mustard Seeds and Spring Onions, 64
- Fresh Cabbage Pancakes, 150
- Green Couscous, 76
- Sweetcorn and Potato Chowder, 134

Stilton Toasts with Roasted Grapes, 110
Sugar Snap Peas, Watercress, and Mint Salad, 72
sweetcorn
- Corn on the Cob with Whipped Honey-Miso Butter, 29
- Sweetcorn and Potato Chowder, 134
- Veggie Chilli-Stuffed Jacket Potatoes, 89

Sweets, Chocolate-Dipped Honeycomb, 17

T
Tea, Haycorn, 59
Thumbprint Biscuits, 49
thyme
- Stilton Toasts with Roasted Grapes, 110
- Sweetcorn and Potato Chowder, 134
- Tomato and Herbed Ricotta Galette, 83

Tigger-Striped Biscuits, 154
Toast, Mushrooms on, 125
tomatoes
- Chilli Cornbread Casserole, 139
- Tomato and Herbed Ricotta Galette, 83
- Veggie Chilli-Stuffed Jacket Potatoes, 89

Trifle, Dirt Cake, 47
Trio of Flavoured Honeys, 21
Trio of Quick Pickles, 90
Trout Dip, Smoked, 63
turkey
- Chilli Cornbread Casserole, 139
- Pooh's Pasties, 153

V
vegetables
- Eeyore's Rainbow Veggie and Hummus Tray, 80
- Roasted Vegetable Platter with Honey Butter Glaze, 119

Veggie Chilli-Stuffed Jacket Potatoes, 89

W
Walnut Baklava, 30
Watercress, and Mint Salad, Sugar Snap Peas, 72
Watermelon, Salted, Punch with Cucumber and Basil, 67
Wedge Salad with Carrot-Ginger Dressing, 71
Witches' Brew, 106

Y
yoghurt
- Coronation Chicken Sliders, 60
- Honeyed Yoghurt Parfait with Quinoa, Pomegranate Seeds, and Grapes, 22
- Za'atar Roasted Chickpeas, Butternut Squash, and Red Onions with Lime Yoghurt, 133

Z
Za'atar Roasted Chickpeas, Butternut Squash, and Red Onions with Lime Yoghurt, 133

PO Box 3088
San Rafael, CA 94912
www.insighteditions.com

◼ Find us on Facebook: www.facebook.com/InsightEditions
◻ Follow us on Instagram: @insighteditions

© 2026 Disney, Based on the 'Winnie the Pooh' works by A.A. Milne and E.H. Shepard

All rights reserved. Published by Insight Editions, San Rafael, California, in 2026.

No part of this book may be reproduced in any form without written permission from the publisher.

UK Edition ISBN: 979-8-3374-0369-4

Publisher: Raoul Goff
SVP, Group Publisher: Vanessa Lopez
VP, Creative: Chrissy Kwasnik
VP, Manufacturing: Alix Nicholaeff
Editorial Director: Thom O'Hearn
Art Director: Stuart Smith
Senior Designer: Judy Wiatrek Trum
Managing Editor: Shannon Ballesteros
Production Editor: Ivy Long
Production Manager: Deena Hashem
Strategic Production Planner: Lina s Palma-Temena

Photographer: Ken Waterbury
Food Stylist: Josh Hake

Insight Editions, in association with Roots of Peace, will plant two trees for each tree used in the manufacturing of this book. Roots of Peace is an internationally renowned humanitarian organisation dedicated to eradicating land mines worldwide and converting war-torn lands into productive farms and wildlife habitats. Roots of Peace will plant two million fruit and nut trees in Afghanistan and provide farmers there with the skills and support necessary for sustainable land use.

Manufactured in China by Insight Editions

10 9 8 7 6 5 4 3 2 1